The Gift of Minimalism
Live More With Less

Simplify, Declutter and Get Organized

By: Karen Alexander

Teresa Baker

ISBN-13: 978-1493714780

COPYRIGHT © 2013 KAREN ALEXANDER

The scanning, copying, uploading and distribution of this book via the Internet or via any other means without the permission of the publisher is not permitted. Please purchase only authorized editions, and do not participate in or encourage electronic piracy of copyrighted materials. Your support of the author's rights and efforts in the publishing of this book is appreciated.

All Rights Reserved

This publication is intended to provide helpful and informative material. The author and publisher specifically disclaim all responsibility for any liability, loss or risk, personal or otherwise, which is incurred as a consequence, directly or indirectly, from the use or application of any contents of this book.

Paperback Edition

Manufactured in the United States of America

To my daughter, Natasha, who proudly proclaimed to her pre-school teacher that her top goal was to organize. I may have chuckled at that time, but she has kept me on my toes ever since and most certainly has taught me a thing or two....

TABLE OF CONTENTS

Introduction   1

PART ONE ▪ CORE PRINCIPLES

1   What Do We Mean By Minimalism   7

2   How Do You Know If Minimalism is Right for You   10

3   Getting Started   18

PART TWO ▪ SKILLS YOU NEED

4   How to Develop Powerful New Habits   23

5   Getting Motivated to Get Things Done   29

6   How to Beat Procrastination   37

7   Defining What Is Necessary   43

8   The IF-THEN Model   49

PART THREE ▪ GETTING IT DONE

9   Declutter and Take Control   55

10   Quick Start Decluttering   60

| 11 | Digging Deeper | 64 |
| 12 | Transition Time | 69 |

PART FOUR ▪ FUNCTIONAL SPACES

13	Common Living Areas	77
14	Kitchen and Pantry	81
15	Bathrooms	88
16	Bedrooms	92
17	Closets and Wardrobes	97

PART FIVE ▪ INTANGIBLES

18	Time Management	105
19	Money Matters	108
20	Life In Balance	117
21	Enjoy the Journey and the Results	121

About the Author

INTRODUCTION

So you've decided enough is enough.

You've been racing through this marathon we call life and are wondering if everything has been worth it. You may have decided that working 60 + hours a week – nights, weekends, during family events or vacations – just is not worth the ability to purchase another one of the 'hottest' electronic gadgets, buy a brand new car and live in enough square feet so that you can acquire, maintain and store more stuff.

You may be someone who has decided that you have lost your keys, missed an appointment, forgotten to pay a bill or spent way too much time searching for something you needed for the very last time.

Maybe you're tired of not getting the chance to sit down and read a good book, watch a movie, have a relaxing meal or spend time with someone you love with no interruptions – or can even remember the last time you did.

Do you feel miserable when you look around at the heaps of clutter, the accumulated 'stuff', and the dust, dirt and utter mess that come along with your possessions?

And more than likely, you want substantially less stress, to find more happiness and fulfillment, and to regain control over your life. Perhaps you haven't even had time to realize until now, just how over-stressed and unhappy you are because you have been multi-tasking and running the rat race.

If any of this sounds familiar to you, it is time to simplify and get organization back into your life. You are not alone in this realization. Many people are saying *enough is enough*. But saying that and knowing what and how to do something about it can seem like a daunting task.

If you have been searching for a way to simplify, organize and maybe even embrace a minimalist style of living then you need to know how to get there. You will need the right training and tools to get the job done, just like anything in life. You didn't learn how to ride a bike without someone teaching you the basics.

Don't fall in to the trap of saying "I'm just a disorganized person" or "Once I get this organized, it only will go back to a cluttered mess after a few weeks anyway". Now you don't have to feel like you can't get organized or simplify your life because you don't know where to begin.

My goal with this book is to get you get past all of these obstacles that have been stopping you in the past. You will first start by **assessing** what is the root cause of why you are disorganized and stressed. You need to understand how you either lost control or how you never quite got there in the first place.

Once you understand the root cause, only then can you make a **realistic plan** to reduce the clutter, get organized and stay that way. You will learn how to make a plan for how to attack the problems and get you to where you want to be.

This whole process comes full circle when you actually use the tools to **get it done** and keep it that way. The fun part happens when you actually see the progress and feel great about what you have accomplished.

My hope is that I can help you make this an easy process and a lifelong skill. Now, let's get started.

PART ONE

CORE PRINCIPLES

> Simplicity is the Ultimate form of Sophistication.
> —Leonardo DaVinci

CHAPTER 1

WHAT DO WE MEAN BY MINIMALISM

Just like many things in our life, minimalism can and does have many definitions and interpretations. For some individuals, minimalism means living with as few possessions as possible. Yet for others minimalism can mean living a simpler, less cluttered life. This lifestyle can include reducing our possessions, freeing up more time, eliminating stress, spending less money and finding contentment.

The concept of minimalism is not a new fad even though it may appear to be from the frequency of articles we see and the discussions taking place. However, minimalism has been around for thousands of years and in varying degrees; from Buddhist Monks to Gandhi to Mother Teresa; Henry David Thoreau during his time at Walden Pond; Coco Chanel's clean and elegant clothing designs; and your Grandparents who lived and survived through the Great Depression. However, we don't have to live on a mountaintop or in a cabin in the woods in order to simplify our lives in a modern-day world.

Minimalist living today, for many of us, is a concentrated reassessment of our values and what is meaningful to us. We need to step back, realign our values and focus on the essential and important things in our life. Because this evaluation is extremely personal, a minimalist lifestyle will be very different for each one of us.

The key to adopting minimalism is to focus on what is important in your life - not the 'stuff', but the 'real' things that bring fulfillment and happiness to your life.

Once we honestly assess and focus upon what is really important to us, then we can begin to eliminate the clutter and stress in our lives.

This book will help you determine what minimalism means to you and how to seamlessly integrate your concept of minimalism or simplifying into your everyday life. I do not intend to coach you into being something you are not. After all, those are the types of things we have tried before to do and that never actually stick.

I'm sure you have all experienced the "lose weight without diet or exercise" or "make money overnight and quit your day job". Perhaps, you have even picked up a magazine or another book on simplifying and organizing that has promised you that you can rid yourself of clutter in a weekend. While those headlines are intriguing, we either don't follow through on the instructions or we fall back to our old habits within a week.

Your self-assessment is the key in determining what level of minimalism and simplicity you want and need in your life. There three broad levels of minimalism that anyone can embrace.

First, you may just be happy by decluttering your living spaces and working areas. This is the basic form of minimalism and the first step to becoming less stressed and re-evaluating what is important to you. This is the materialistic evaluation stage of minimalism.

If you have eliminated the first type of clutter and disorganization from your life, you may decide to just stop there or you may want to evaluate and eliminate the excesses that still rob you of your freedom. These are the types of things that rob you of your time because you need to work more or harder to pay for them and then to manage them along the way. They include things like cable subscriptions, club memberships, magazine, impulse purchases, installment payment plans, and cell phone plans.

In the final bucket is the more extreme and philosophical form of minimalism. This is the type that quite often gives the term minimalism a bad rap. You decide to quit your job, sell most of your things and live very sparsely. Like anything in life, politics, religion, diet and health, there are the extremists. If that works for you fine, but that is not the type of minimalism that we will be referring to throughout this book.

Simplicity, organization, minimalism or whatever you choose to call it, is a step toward eliminating clutter, reducing stress and saving money. Why do I call Minimalism a gift? That is because it enables you to free up your time to do the things you love, be happier and get more fulfillment out of your life. What better gift is there than that...

CHAPTER 2

HOW DO YOU KNOW IF MINIMALISM IS RIGHT FOR YOU

Minimalism is right for you if your heart longs for a simpler lifestyle uncluttered with stuff you do not really need. When trying to decide if you want to explore the concept of minimalism, allow your intuition to persuade your mind that a less complex way of living may help you feel less stress and more alive.

It is important to remember that your way of approaching minimalism is not necessarily the same as another person's method. You do not need to sell your house and live as in a cabin in the woods in order to embrace the minimalist philosophy that promotes living an uncomplicated lifestyle.

You are ready for more minimalism and simplicity if any, or many, of these sound familiar to you.

- You look at your surroundings and feel overwhelmed by the amount of stuff you see.

- You are constantly searching for your keys or an important piece of paper.

- It takes you what seems like forever to pick up and clean your house periodically.

- You like clean and tidy rooms but don't like to clean.

- You are in a rush every morning to find something to wear. Once your finally pick the right outfit you realize something isn't cleaned or you have to dig through your room or closet to find the right pair of shoes that goes with it.

- You look at your savings or checking account and wonder where all the money goes to every month.

- You have missed appointments, meetings, or kids soccer games because you forgot the time and date or were too with other things.

- You are exhausted by the hours you work or don't feel fulfilled by the work you do.

- You don't invite friends over because your house is such a mess.

- You have items in your closet, drawers or cabinets that you haven't worn or touched in years.

- You are moving and deep down you know it doesn't make sense to move ever item you currently own.

Who Doesn't Want Less Stress

One reason for embracing minimalism is that you will experience less stress and a greater sense of inner peace, both of which are good for your body and mind.

Just picture for a moment you are walking up to a friend's house. One house has toys scattered in the yard, there are empty planters, rakes and brooms stacked near the garage, and when you look at the open garage you wonder how they even get a car in there. Now you visit your other friend's house. The house has clean and simple lines, the yard is clear or clutter and the front porch has one tasteful piece of art. What do you feel as you approach each house? At the first house you most likely feel more anxious and stressed before you even arrive at the door. At the second house, you feel calm and less stress. You even feel better about going in to the house. In reality, minimalism is less stressful and much more calming.

When you own less material items and eliminate unnecessary activities, you have more time to appreciate your family, friends and simple things in life.

Think about how many hours have you may have spent cleaning out your garage or basement. Does this give you satisfaction? Sure. Would you have been more satisfied if you could have been doing something fun, like participating in your favorite pastime or playing with your kids? Absolutely! If you didn't have so many possessions and 'stuff' you could readily be doing more enjoyable activities – the ones that really matter to you.

However, you do not need to live in sparse surroundings without furniture, books, DVDs or a television set. If these items give you pleasure than by all means keep them.

Simplicity is all about being able to live with the things and do the things that make you happy. However, you need to be honest with yourself about just exactly what these things are.

Keep the Stuff that Helps you Live a more Significant Lifestyle

The main idea behind minimalism is to weed out the items that tend to take you away from your purpose in life. If watching a documentary or uplifting movie helps you live a more fulfilled life, then you do not need to throw the videos away or donate them to a charitable organization.

On the other hand, if you are in the habit of watching movies or television programs just because you don't want to tackle the real issues in life, you may want to consider giving up these detrimental habits.

Set Each Goal One Step at a Time

If you want to live your life as a minimalist, create one goal at a time. If you try to create too many goals at once, you are contradicting the essence of minimalism, which serves to make you confused and resentful. If you are ready to simplify and are willing to follow a proven process then you will have a much greater chance of reaching your goal.

Often, when we decide to tackle a new concept such as minimalism, we jump in feet first without really assessing and planning what and how we can accomplish our goal. When you do this, your chances of success are limited. And even worse, if you do achieve some sort of simplicity you will most likely fall back into your old habits.

Change your Views about 'Stuff'

You will need to be ready to look at your possessions with a critical eye. If you are ready to tackle this issue – and it often can be a stumbling block – then you are much closer to embracing minimalism.

This doesn't mean that we will tell you to get rid of everything that you haven't worn in a year, or your kid's old artwork or even the multitude of kitchen gadgets we can acquire. What this does mean is that you will need to look at each one of these items and determine if it really does have a place in your life right now.

When loved one passes away or a relationship ends, we often keep many of the things that remind us of this person or that time in our life. These items can have real meaning for us and then by all means keep them. However, if you can make a determination that some of these items bring us sadness or we keep them out of guilt, then you need to find a path to get rid of them.

Don't Get Drawn In By Commercialism

Watch television commercials or read magazines, and you are likely to think you need an excessive amount of gadgets, trinkets or the latest model to feel happy. The truth is that happiness does not stem from material possessions, but from a deeper part of you that feels content with simple things.

If you can remind yourself that this form of marketing comes solely from a company's goal to make money and not from reality, then you will be able to make a better decision about whether or not an purchase will really add more value to your inner self.

For example, do you really need the latest phone, pc, tablet or toy? Will making a choice to purchase these only serve to get money out of your pocket and not satisfaction back into your life? If you can even pause just a moment to make this evaluation, chances are you will be closer to living more simply. If you have recently purchased a new cellphone or tech gadget and then found out that the 'latest and greatest' model is coming out in a month, then you know the feeling of how short term your pleasure and satisfaction are from consumption.

The myth of needs purported by advertisers is often far from the reality of needs for our happiness.

Live a Healthier Lifestyle

If you are ready to feel better both inside and out, then minimalism is a choice you should make. Learn to appreciate the wonders of nature and the simplicity of going on early morning walks. View squirrels and birds instead of daytime television. Eliminate costly and unhealthy junk foods. Eat a simple, healthy diet consisting of whole grains, beans, yogurt, fresh fruits and fresh vegetables. Take a yoga class or learn to meditate. Learn to take slow, deep breaths and you can clean your mind and your body.

A Minimalist is not an Extremist

The author Charles Dickens wrote about a miser named Ebenezer Scrooge in his novel *A Christmas Tale*. Please note that there is a difference between living the lifestyle of a miser and living the life of a minimalist. Prior to his spiritual awakening, the character Ebenezer Scrooge lived an empty and meaningless life centered on his miserly nature that reeked of selfish motives. The philosophy of minimalism focuses on living a more unselfish and spiritually gratifying life.

St. Francis of Assisi was a Famous Spiritual Minimalist too. The beloved Roman Catholic saint set an example for all future generations about how to live a simple lifestyle as a minimalist. In the famous book *The Little Flowers of St. Francis of Assisi*, the saint's followers wrote that he would get angry whenever he saw a person who led a more impoverished lifestyle than the life he was living. Stories depict St. Francis begging for food and using a big stone for his pillow.

You do not need to be a miser, use a rock for your pillow, or sleep on a bed made from straw, if you want to live your life as a minimalist.

But if you want to experience your life in a new and positive way, consider your options of living as a minimalist and the tremendous benefits that come with this lifestyle.

Getting this Done Right

If you are looking for the perfect answer or the quick and easy solution, you need to know that none exists. What can be perfect for one person just will not work for another. There are as many ways to get organized as people that want to get organized.

How you get this done right is to find a system that will work for you. Most importantly, you need a system that you honestly feel good about and one that you can stick to. If you are constantly starting and stopping new systems that someone has told you about, then you are most likely disheartened, frustrated and worst of all…still unorganized.

Be cautious of getting caught in analysis-paralysis or waiting to find the perfect solution. Just pick a process and start. If you're not sure of which system to use, pick one you think may work for you and follow it for one month. At the end of the month you can make adjustments if something isn't working – but at least you have a realistic example to work from and one that is unique to you.

In order accomplish your goal of simplifying and getting organized, I will give you tools and tips to help you evaluate your situation, make a plan for change, and then get it done. There are two critical steps to before you can even begin to start simplifying and decluttering.

You will need to determine the cause of your clutter and disorganization. Once you have a better handle on this, you will find it much easier to tackle your issues.

You will also need to determine your goals. Do you want to have more time, more money, less stress, more happiness, or just get rid of junk. Understanding standing what you want out of this will help you make a plan and measure your results.

If your happiness is threatened by clutter, you need to make the conscious decision to live a minimalist lifestyle that emphasizes owning less stuff and getting what you do own organized.

So I'm hoping by now, you understand that I'm not going to ask you to jump off of the deep end into the dark abyss of minimalism. Nor am I going to tell you to do something that isn't right for you.

What I will ask you to do and help you to do is to learn how to make changes, embrace new habits, and stay motivated to simplify and get organized. Now that you know what to expect, we will get started with utilizing some tools to make this process right for you and remarkably doable.

CHAPTER 3

GETTING STARTED

So now you have decision time. You are motivated to get started and you have the tools available to start organizing and decluttering your life. Get ready to utilize the skills we talked about in the previous chapters regarding developing good habits and defining what is necessary and meaningful to you.

As we go through our home and our schedules we will be making decisions about what is necessary and what is important to us. But what happens when we take a look around and it seems that everything in our line of sight is important to us.

At this point, we really need to be questioning everything that we own. We need to pick up, touch, 'talk to' and evaluate each and every piece. Now this may first appear like this task will take up a lot of unnecessary time. However if we don't truly evaluate and make a decision about each and every piece, we run the risk of just putting an unnecessary item back in the same spot or just storing it. After all, that is one of the reasons we ended up here in the first place.

Over the years, I had acquired many things and put them in a specific place. I cleaned around them and occasionally moved them ever so slightly to make room for something else. What happens here is we become immune to their existence and value. The items around us become almost transparent. We really don't 'see' them…they are just *there*. So when you think about it in that way, does it really make sense to keep them? Would you take them with you if there was a fire in your home – ok maybe that's a little extreme – but would you even notice them if they were missing?

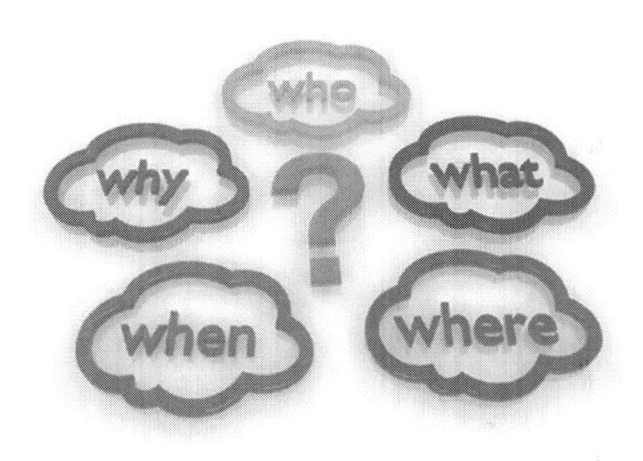

Try this: take a look – a real hard look - at the items in your line of site right now. If you see 10 items that are really important to you and are necessary, congratulations! However if you are like many of us, you most likely are staring at 50 items. Some of these items may have great value to you. But the remainder is likely knick-knacks that we acquired along the way or were given to us – and when asked, we probably couldn't find a really good reason why we still have them.

There also might be items that we don't even need to take time to evaluate. These items could be things that we haven't put back in their proper place and are now cluttering another area – old magazines,

GETTING STARTED | 19

receipts, empty glasses and a host of other items that we set down and either don't throw away or don't put back in their proper place.

Pick up one item in your line of site that you may have received as a gift or picked up on one of your vacations. Does this item remind you of the person who gifted it to you or the trip you took? Is that the only reason you would remember that person or event – I think not. So if you removed this item from its current spot and either gave it away, threw it away or put it into a storage box, would you miss looking at it every day? Would you feel badly that it was no longer there? If so, then by all means keep it. However if you remove it and you don't even notice that it is missing, is it really worth keeping? Better yet, if you remove that item would you have more open space, less to clean and therefore a little more time? Would it help you to live in the present and look ahead to the future versus clinging on to the past?

If you can do this evaluation every time you handle an item, you will be well on your way to simplifying your life and living with less. Now this may seem like it could be a long and arduous process if you have to do this with every item. Trust me you won't. There will be items you will know immediately what to do with them. Also, remember the adage 'practice makes perfect'. The more you do this with each item, the more practiced you will get at it and the faster subsequent tasks will happen. It does really get easier and easier. Don't lose your motivation. Remind yourself of your goals. Enjoy the process and know that the power of habit will soon make this easy for you to help you achieve your objectives.

PART TWO

SKILLS YOU NEED

> It is our choices that
> show what we truly are,
> far more than our abilities.
> — J. K. Rowling

CHAPTER 4

HOW TO DEVELOP POWERFUL NEW HABITS

If your home is filled with stuff, you are likely to feel stressed out by the clutter. Your immediate physical surroundings, to a certain degree, reflect your inner self and mind.

If you feel you are constantly on a frantic schedule, are always running late and have way too many things to handle, then you are also negatively impacted by your time clutter.

There are indeed many reasons for allowing clutter to dominate your home environment and life. Some of these reasons are non-threatening things we can change or control. Other reasons can be outside ourselves – these are still things that we can change, but we will have to reach outside to fix them or to ask for help. Still others may result from a deep seated physiological or psychological deterrence. This is probably the most difficult one to change but not impossible.

If you are depressed because you recently lost a loved one or job, you may compensate your loss by shopping and buying stuff you do not really need to own.

Perhaps you lack energy because of an unhealthy lifestyle, and you simply do not have the momentum to take care of the clutter problem.

Surrounding yourself with clutter may help you think you can cope with depression, loneliness or unhappiness when in fact is maybe one of the roots causes of your feelings.

Too much clutter can also be caused by simple reasons, such as the fear of not being able to find items in your closet or on your desk when you need them.

You may lack ample storage space for the items you possess. If you recently moved to a new home, you may feel overwhelmed by all the boxes and simply allow them to rest comfortably on your living room floor for an unlimited amount of time.

You need to find out the reasons for your obsession with clutter. Once you understand your motives, it is easier to eliminate or change the habit.

How to Develop a Habit that Opposes Collecting Stuff

Owning too much stuff causes clutter, especially if you live in a smaller home without enough closet and storage space. One way to get rid of the habit that has caused an abundance of clutter in your house or apartment is to develop a new habit that contradicts your desire to collect stuff.

In order to eliminate the old habit and you will need a certain amount of patience and determination during the process. By definition, a habit is created by repeatedly doing the same thing. Since we only have so much available time and energy, we will replace our clutter habit with a newer more beneficial habit.

This is a common approach to making positive changes – replace an old negative habit with a new habit that is counter to your old habit. For example when people try to quit smoking, they are encouraged to start a healthy activity such as walking or exercising that they enjoy. It's hard to enjoy a good walk if you are having trouble breathing from smoking – you're also not inclined to light a cigarette if you are on a nice brisk walk.

FOLLOW
ONE
COURSE
UNTIL
SUCCESSFUL

Replace your Old Habit with a New Habitual Response

The best way to get rid of a negative habit that interferes with your spiritual happiness is to stop participating in the habit. While the practice is easier said than done, you can succeed by having a goal. Write your goal down in a notebook dedicated to your new minimalist lifestyle. Apply willpower and determination to refrain from collecting stuff that clutters your home. Stop going to yard sales or other habitual clutter haunts.

If you bring the mail into your house and always throw it on the same pile, try coming in the door and immediately opening your mail and throwing away the junk. Then place the important pieces in a file or inbox.

One of my worst clutter problems was the piles and piles of mail that I would receive and just pile. I missed bill payments and important notices like car registrations and things for my daughter's school. To add to the problem, the piles of mail started to take up valuable space and collect dust. I was disgusted and annoyed by it. Unfortunately the more disgusted I got, the more I avoided the piles. Until one day, I decided enough was enough. I cleared through the existing piles and established a new habit. Now when I bring in the mail each and every piece is dealt with immediately. Either thrown out – actually a large amount of stuff falls into this category - or put in a nice 'to do' folder. I effectively replaced an unproductive habit with a new organized habit. The feeling has been entirely liberating and I no longer have any issues from things I didn't deal with appropriately.

How to Eliminate the Habit of Collecting Stuff

Instead of collecting stuff that turns into clutter, develop a new minimalist attitude that favors a simple lifestyle. If you have a strong determination to live a life centered on simplicity, then you will start to develop a new and stronger habit that replaces your old way of thinking about stuff.

Refer back to my example of quitting smoking. Another great tool that is encouraged to help people quit is to avoid the locations and activities that trigger their urge to smoke. I worked for an individual who always smoked sitting at his desk in his office while he was on the phone– yes that was quite a few years ago. When he was quitting smoking, he made all of his phone calls sitting in a guest chair on the exact opposite side of his desk. Just such a simple change of position, eliminated the habit trigger of him wanting to light a cigarette.

Simple change – amazing results. That is what we use to encourage ourselves to eliminate a habit. The level of energy required to make the change can be so simple compared to the extraordinary benefits that result. Remind yourself of the benefits and the changes will come easier.

If you are prone to follow all the sales that you see advertised and then shop those sales, you can readily be encouraged to buy things that you do not need and will end up being clutter. While looking for items on sale is a good thing, looking for sales is not. When we actually need something and look for a sale price we save ourselves money. When we look for a sale and then just buy because it is on sale, we are spending money unnecessarily and we are acquiring things that we don't need.

The next time you are confronted with this choice, look hard at the item you are thinking of buying. Stop and ask yourself a some questions. Do I really *need* this item – not just *want* this item – but *need* this item? Chances are the wants are what got you into a cluttered state in the first place. Will this item make me happy? Not just happy now, but for a long time. Does this item fit into my goals of living simpler? Does this item satisfy some true needs that I have? Will this contribute to my health or sense of well-being?

Eventually, you will lose the desire to look for items you do not really need, and you will prefer living in an uncluttered atmosphere. You will begin to appreciate uncluttered rooms and your home's peaceful environment. Lack of clutter may even cause you to feel less stressful about other issues going on in your life. Simplicity and serenity are close friends of minimalism.

Minimalism and Simplicity Doesn't Just Include 'Stuff'

Exploring minimalism opens new avenues to contemplate that include financial matters. In addition to eliminating clutter, you may want to stop spending too much money on things that cause you to lead an unhealthy and unwholesome lifestyle. Buy a special notebook in which you can write down all your purchases for the next three months. After the end of the three-month period, study your notebook. You will readily see which items you need and those you do not need to buy. Once you understand your habitual spending habits, you can stop buying unnecessary items, and substitute them for things that help you live your life in a simple and healthy way.

Have you been asked by someone to go somewhere, do something or help out at an event and later regretted your decision? We often react to requests by a friend, family member or associate with a quick response. We don't take into account what this could do to clutter up our schedule even more. Again, pause before answering or acting. Ask yourself if this will just put more stress and clutter into your life or if this will actually have some meaningful benefit.

Remember that your approach to minimalism is not the same as your neighbor's path. There are indeed very different types of minimalists and a variety of approaches to minimalism. Each person has different needs, wants and goals. Your particular approach is the only one that counts.

Use your Imagination to Accomplish your Dreams

If your life does not reflect your dreams about how you want to live, allow your imagination to inspire you. Follow the dictates of your heart. Your inner self will direct you toward the minimalist path that is right for you. If you long for a simpler and more serene lifestyle, you are taking the right steps.

CHAPTER 5

GETTING MOTIVATED TO GET THINGS DONE

Achieving your goals is about figuring out what you want and then motivating yourself to get there. It is also about keeping your focus on that goal and keeping yourself motivated. Read through the list of motivation tips and factors here. Think about how each one of them can work for you. You don't have to embrace all of them. The last thing I want you to do is make more work out of the process instead of achieving your goal.

Just know that these are established motivational steps. Use them to keep you motivated toward your goals.

1. Think positive. I know this may sound very cliché, but in reality this method just plain works! Think about the present and your current goals. Don't focus on the past and keep bringing up old, negative thoughts. Continuing to dwell on your past problems will not help you with the present. So push those negative thoughts out!

Think about the positive things you are trying to accomplish. It can be very helpful to say your new positive thoughts out loud...and repeat them. There is something about vocalizing them that reaffirms their value to us. Also, when you are saying a positive thought, it takes the space and energy of the negative thoughts. Try it. Do it daily. Especially do this when a negative thought enters your conscious. Soon you will have a stream of positive thoughts to keep you motivated.

2. Set mini goals and long term goals. It is much easier to tackle little pieces that it is to try to tackle a seemingly monumental task. The expression, "You can't see the forest through the trees' is very real when it comes to achieving your goals. If your goal seems too overwhelming, break it apart into small chunks or mini-goals. It is much easier to understand how to do a small goals and tasks. You will find the long term goal becomes more manageable. Plus you will get the added benefit of rewarding yourself for achieving milestones.

3. Keep a daily list, calendar, journal, or whatever recording means works for you. Just make sure that whatever you are planning on using to set your goals is something you are actually comfortable using. Nothing is more defeating than not being able to keep up with your record keeping methods. Make sure you record things as they happen. Don't wait until the end of the day and then try to remember them. It can be particularly useful to note if this was easy or hard and the factors that lead you to complete - or not complete - them. At the end of the week, take a look at your weeks' worth of activities. For goals that you didn't meet, transfer them over to next week and make adjustments if necessary.

4. Have meaningful and powerful reasons. Again, write them down. These should be goals that really motivate you and will make an important difference in your life. If you are doing this to help yourself or your family members, that can be extremely powerful. Much more powerful than saying you want to buy yourself a new pair of shoes. If you desperately want to achieve something, your ability to keep yourself motivated becomes much easier.

5. Visualize your goals. Do this daily. Doing this first thing in the morning is especially useful. You can visualize your goal, firmly plant it in your brain and start your day off motivated. If you can, take a picture of something that you are trying to achieve and tape it to your wall. If a picture doesn't make sense, then just write out your goal in big letters put it in a visible place. Take time in your day to look at your goal or motivational picture. Do this for at least 5 minutes. Take time to absorb all the feelings and senses you will experience by reaching your goal. Make a clear mental picture of your goal. How will you feel? What will you hear? What will you smell, taste? All of these senses help you to really see your goal as a reality. Do this activity daily or multiple times a day until you firmly implant it into your mind and heart. This process will help keep you motivated through difficult times. It also has the benefit of allowing you to make adjustments without completely giving up.

6. Keep track of your progress. Write things down that you have accomplished. Cross items off of your to-do list. I love to do this! Such a simple movement a crossing something off a list can have such an exhilarating effect. Not only does it feel good, it motivates me to tackle the next item on the list. This is also a great way to keep track of what you need to do yet and where you are in your progress toward your end goal.

Some individuals like journals or charts to keep track. Something that we have been conditioned to appreciate since childhood is getting a gold star. Put one of those on your calendar every time you make a step toward you goal. These seemingly little stars are a great visual reward! Find what works best for you to track your progress and keep you motivated. Whatever you choose to do, give yourself a reward and enjoy the moment!

There will be times - and be ready for them - where you didn't earn all gold stars. Just remind yourself that that is not a reason to give up. It's a minor bump in the road compared to the feeling you will have from reaching your goal. Just learn from it and move on.

7. Make slow and measurable progress. Whenever I set a new goal, I am over-the-top motivated to dive right in. This initial enthusiasm is good for anyone as long as you don't go overboard at the onset.

When I start a new goal or project, I am ready to go all out! But I don't always put the reins on... I am embarrassed to say how many incomplete craft projects I use to have sitting around the house. The problem for me was I would choose the biggest and most difficult project to tackle! I would go out immediately and acquire all the things I thought I would need. The problem was, I occasionally would become frustrated, unable or unwilling to complete what I had started.

Stumbling blocks to accomplish our goals happens to all of us because we run out of time or our enthusiasm fades. To make matters worse, once you think about or see these incomplete projects or goals on your horizon it can be even more demotivating.

So bottom-line - don't jump in head first - take it slowly and methodically so you can see some motivating results! Once I see a small project finished, I am even more energized and motivated to tackle the next one.

8. Start. Yup that's it...start. I know that may sound trite. But you really need to just get going and start somewhere. Don't worry about it being perfect, especially for the first time through. Don't fall into the perfectionist trap - where you can't begin something until everything is just right. You will spend more time looking for perfectionism that you would have spent just getting started on your project or goal.

If you keep pondering what you need to accomplish, you will exhaust yourself. The task is rarely as hard as you thought it was going to be. If, once you start, it is a little overwhelming, don't get discouraged. Just break it down into smaller, more manageable pieces. Just don't waste precious time and energy 'thinking' about it. Just start.

9. Make it fun. If you are sorting and organizing drawers, turn on some high energy music that you like to keep you going. If you are trying to clear up your calendar, enjoy the pure and utter satisfaction that comes from saying 'no'. You and your coworkers or others in your life, will soon begin to realize that they really didn't 'need' to sponge up so much time. It's a liberating feeling!

10. Reward yourself. This all comes down to human nature. If you can reward yourself for each and every accomplishment, you are much more motivated to continue. Establish what your mini-rewards will be. Make them comparable to the size of the goal. Make sure you have them written down, just like you have your goals written down. This way, when the time comes, you know exactly what you can treat yourself with. Just make sure your reward isn't counterproductive to the goal you are trying to achieve. If you are trying to declutter your kitchen, don't reward yourself by going out and buying that new kitchen gadget you have been dreaming about.

11. Be patient. In this age of immediate gratification, this may be a skill you have to relearn. You didn't get where you are today overnight. Then why think you can fix it overnight. Most things that are worth having are worth waiting for. The goal you established for yourself is no different. If you want to clean out that closet, just remember it didn't get that way overnight. Also keep in mind that once you have this project completed, you won't have to tackle it again. That is of course if you don't fall back into the same trap. I always tell myself, I can do just about anything for an hour - or whatever timeframe I choose - because at the end of that hour it will be all done and I will feel great. You will get results if you embrace what I am telling you and follow along with these tools.

12. Get encouragement. There are few things more powerful that getting encouragement from people you love and respect. If you have

told your family or friends about your new goal, then also fill them in on your progress. If a photo, poster or inspirational saying helps you stay motivated, then take the time to explore these. If you want to get new ideas for your new minimalist lifestyle, then join a group or an online forum for inspiring stories.

13. Avoid getting derailed or sidetracked. You will have urges to give up. We all do. You just need to be aware of this and be ready to act upon (deal with)it. Stop and think about the places or triggers that might be waiting out there to demotivate you. Then have a plan of attack. One of the best ways for overcoming this urge is to have a plan in place to deal with it. Write down your plan. Make it a visual just like your goals are and then implement your plan. When I was quitting smoking a number of years ago, I wrote down the places and times I might have the greatest urge to smoke a cigarette. The odd thing about this was that some places and situations I hadn't even considered would set off a trigger. My written down plan for dealing with the situations I had anticipated also worked for me for the unanticipated times. If I hadn't had a plan written down, I am sure I could have been derailed for my goal much easier.

14. Don't be a Superhero. Don't give up on your long term goal just because you didn't accomplish all your goals this week or lost your motivation. We are not Superheroes. Things happen that can take us off course. So what if you didn't accomplish something. Just do it another day or time. Or get yourself back on track. A little tumble is not worth giving up on your goals entirely. Remind yourself - and visualize - why you started this in the first place. You will be happy you didn't give up!

15. Create a little competition. If you are trying to declutter or not accumulate more clutter in your home or on your schedule, you can easily make this a 'friendly' competition among family members. Most people love a little challenge. The best part about this is that is gets others in your household engaged in your goals too. Just make sure your competition is positive and doesn't turn into a 'you didn't do that fiasco'. Those types of engagements only produce negative effects. Certainly something we want to stay away from. So have a little fun. Engage others. And get ready to spur yourself on.

16. Proclaim your new goals from the mountain top! Well not 'exactly' that...but the idea is to tell your friends and family about your new goals. Fully commit yourself. This method works time and time again. Your friends and family can hold you accountable. You can even ask for their help! There is nothing like telling others that will make you believe in your goals too.

17. Don't let in negative thoughts. Don't tell yourself that you lack discipline or that you have never been an organized person. If something doesn't work out the way you planned, make adjustments and move on. Don't stop. Look at it as a little detour. Tell yourself that this is a good thing and that your end result will be just that much better.

One of the things that is important to me is to have time to do the things I want to do. And not feel guilty about it! This could be anything from getting together with family and friends, attending a sporting event, seeing a movie, reading a good book, cooking a fabulous meal, knitting a sweater and sitting on the patio with a cool drink and clearing my mind.

However, if I have spent my day by not doing things at the top of my to-do list I feel guilty taking some relaxation time to do the things I love. Or, if I have lost time dealing with constant interruptions that I didn't manage well and got sidetracked, I feel drained and unmotivated to engage in a fun activity.

I have learned to organize and declutter my belongings and free up my time. Once you get on top of your clutter, the feeling is exuberating. I also know that maintaining control and staying organized is an ongoing process. But once you have things under control, keeping up with it is so much easier and the benefits are worth it!

CHAPTER 6

HOW TO BEAT PROCRASTINATION

Why does this behavior get to so many of us. We have things we know we need to get done, but it is so hard to get started. Doing the laundry, cleaning the house, a report at work and income taxes all are tasks I am sure many of us have put off at one time or another. We all know that these things need to be done, but for some inexplicable reason we avoid getting started.

So let's break down this monster called procrastination. Just telling ourselves to 'not procrastinate' doesn't do the trick. If we can get to the root case, we can tackle it head on and likely eliminate it. When we really don't like to do something we procrastinate. It seems we have convinced ourselves that it will be more painful or annoying to do any given task then to do nothing at all. So how do we get ourselves past this way of thinking.

Procrastinating the Dreadful Tasks

There are certain things we all hate doing. For me the top of the list is doing income taxes. Running a close second is dusting. How about you? What are the things you dread doing the most? Chances are these things are shared by many of us. The question is how do we get past this point and just get it done.

We begin thinking that this task will be more miserable to do than not doing anything at all. We convince ourselves that we find more pleasure in not doing the dreaded task. The best way to change this habit is to change the way we think about it. We need to reverse our thinking and start associating more satisfaction from doing it than the pleasure we derive from avoiding the task.

I have heard many times the suggestion that you should do your most dreaded task first thing in the morning. You will have your worst thing done and then you won't be able to procrastinate. Every task you have for the rest of the day is something more enjoyable. If think this may work for you, give it a try.

However, for me this suggestion has almost the reverse affect. If my most dreaded task is first thing in the morning, I find myself dreading to get up because that is what I have to work on first thing. I then transfer my procrastination of the task to procrastinating getting up. Be careful that you don't give up what bad habit only to replace it by another. I also find that my best time for accomplishing things is early in the day. Tasks you dread often require more energy – either emotional or physical – to get them done. If I use a lot of energy on a task I hate doing early in the day, then I am spent to accomplish better tasks later on.

Alternatively what works better for me is to set a deadline or a specific time that is not first thing in the day. For example, I tell myself that the dreaded task will be started at 3 p.m. or it will be accomplished by 4 p.m. Or I can't leave my office or house until this task is completed. I am always motivated to go on to doing more fun things and that is what keeps me on track.

Here are some tips for attacking this type of procrastination:

1. Visualize the satisfaction you will feel once you have completed the task. It is stressful to be constantly thinking about having to get something done. Think strongly about the good feeling you will have once you have completed your goal. Remind yourself of how less stressful you will feel and how you will have more time to think about the positive things you enjoy doing.

Life Begins at the end of your Comfort Zone

2. Find one thing that will make the task more enjoyable and less painful. This could be anything from giving yourself a reward when you complete the task or finding fulfillment from completing the task. Completing the task could also result in pain avoidance - such as not completing our income taxes! The task itself is not dreadful it is how we perceive the task. Change your perception. If you can find a reward at the end of the task, latch on to that reward. Once we actually dive into a task, we often find that it really isn't as dreadful as we built it up to be.

3. Break your task in to smaller pieces. Often a task seems so overwhelming or time consuming that we just don't want to begin. If you can carve out 30 minutes, you can get a good head start on your project. At the end of the 30 minutes, if you are still motivated keep forging on. If not, give yourself a reward for doing what you have accomplished. Just make sure you purposefully set up another time block to work on it again.

Procrastinating Difficult or Time Consuming Tasks

This type of procrastination occurs because we aren't really sure how to accomplish our project or we have no idea how long it could possibly take us. Projects where we don't have the skills fall into this category. We can also run in to this when we don't think we have the time available to ever accomplish this goal.

There are two good ways to solve this type of procrastination.

1. Make a Plan. Break down the project into smaller tasks. Write each of these down. Make a plan on how and when you will accomplish each task. Smaller, manageable bites will make any task easier.

2. Get Help. Find a great resource such as a friend, family member, or colleague. Ask for help from these individuals. People are typically willing to share knowledge or help someone out. You may need to gather manuals, buy or rent a book, or search for instructions online. Do whatever it takes to help you get off the starting block.

Procrastinating Change

This type of procrastination is one of the hardest to manage and overcome. Change can be incredibly hard to deal with because it often involves a fundamental part of our life. These are not always easy for us to change.

Think of things like moving to another home or city, a career change, quitting a bad habit, or leaving a relationship. None of these are easy to do and are often some of life's biggest events. Making a change in any of these areas takes much more effort and can be very stressful.

However, not making a change can cause stress also. And, while it can take more effort, the feeling from releasing ourselves from an undesirable situation can be very exhilarating.

The first critical phase is to analyze and accept that you have a need for change. We should be truthful with ourselves that we are afraid of making a change. Be honest in accepting that the fear - and only that - is what is causing you to procrastinate.

Once we honestly embrace that we need to make a change, only then are we able to move forward.

1. Tackle the risk factors. Make a list of the pros and cons of making a change and moving forward. Don't get caught up in the 'what if' scenario. By this I mean that we should avoid the tendency to get caught up in all the 'terrible' things that could happen. Instead focus on the positive outcomes. Quiet your perfectionist voice. Sorry folks, but nothing will ever be perfect. If we wait for this to happen, we can be waiting forever.

2. Get support. You can find support from friends, family, physicians, colleagues or support groups. The kind of change you are seeking to make will determine where you find support. Just make sure that the people you choose and the support you get will be the ones that help you move forward. Don't knowingly or subconsciously seek help from those you know will confirm not making a change.

3. Educate yourself. Research your topic or seek professional help. Arming yourself with knowledge is a powerful force to help you. The more knowledge and resources you have, the more confident you will be to move forward.

Procrastination comes in many forms. It can be different for all of us. What is important here is to recognize what the root cause of your procrastination is and deal with that aspect head on.

Reverse the pain vs. gain dynamic. Move yourself to believing that the benefits from acting will be greater than the pain from not doing anything at all. To get the benefits of simplifying your life and reducing stress, overcoming procrastination is a critical component. Take control and the minimalist lifestyle will become a reality.

CHAPTER 7

DEFINING WHAT IS NECESSARY

In order to simplify your belongings, you need to define what you feel is necessary for your new minimalist lifestyle. Like many things in life, what is necessary to each and every one of us can vary significantly.

The answer to this question can change over time depending upon factors in our life such as moving, loss of a family member, an illness, a new baby, loss of job or any number of typical life occurrences. So the answer to the question of what is necessary will be different for everyone reading this book.

The answer to this question will also be determined by how you define 'necessary'. And to really make this work for you...be honest. Only if you are honest will you be even close to getting the benefits of minimalism.

There are two levels of **necessary** that you need to define for yourself. The first level is a broader more holistic definition and relates to your overall goal setting.

The best way that I have found to establish what is necessary to me is to answer the question in a positive statement versus a negative statement. Doing so will set you up for more positive results and not feel like a negative. For example, instead of saying 'I don't have enough time for things I enjoy doing' you should say 'I need or want more time to do things I enjoy'. See the difference? The second statement puts a positive spin on your goal and sets you up better to deal with each item of clutter in your life.

Your answer to the question about what is necessary for you may look something like this:

- I want to spend more time doing things (be specific here) that I like to do.
- I want to reduce the hours that I work.
- I need to improve my health.
- I want to not feel so stressed out by my busy schedule.
- I want to increase my self-confidence.
- I want to get rid of this unnecessary 'stuff'.
- I want to be able to find my keys or an important document when I need it.
- I want to have 15 more minutes to sleep in the morning or have a nice breakfast.
- I need to save money to send my kids to college.
- I want to move to a smaller/larger space.
- I want to invite people over and not feel embarrassed by my living space.

You will need to determine exactly what you want and need. These are just some examples, but they should give you some ideas to get you started.

You need to reach inside yourself and find out what is important and necessary to you. Your definition of necessary doesn't have to be just about material things it could be something intrinsic, emotional or physical. It is all about finding out what brings meaning to you – your trigger point – your hot button – or whatever gets you motivated.

For me, simplifying my life and reducing clutter was necessary to restore my self-esteem.

I had helped my daughter get ready for college, moved into a smaller home, put some things into storage - no make that a lot of things into storage - and still had way too many items for my current space. I also had a tendency to 'pile' things and tell myself that I would deal with them later. 'Later' didn't always happen…

Every time I looked around my living space I could see way too many piles and random items sitting around…and the dust and disarray that come with that. I was getting concerned that the dust bunnies would take on a life of their own!

To make matters worse, my daughter is allergic to dust. So every time she came home, she was constantly blowing her nose and rubbing her eyes. She was miserable and so was I.

When I looked at this 'stuff', I felt overwhelmed. I didn't feel productive. And I certainly didn't feel very good about myself. So for my purposes, getting my life back meant getting rid of stuff – lots of stuff. So with this definition in mind, I could begin to look at my possessions and clutter in an entirely new light.

The next stage then becomes looking at all the items you own and determining if they are necessary to your overall goals and definition of necessary.

How Do You Define What Is Necessary and Make Appropriate Decisions

First, learn to discern between necessities and luxuries, and you are on your way to living a minimalist lifestyle. If you want to learn how to live as a minimalist, you first need to think about your life and the type of lifestyle that fits in with your personality. For instance, if you play professional baseball for a living, you are obviously not going to give up the sport to live your life as a minimalist. Instead, you will think about other things you do not really need. Although deciding what you need is not necessarily easy, you can make a more informed decision if you take stock of what you own.

Create an Activities Inventory

This won't be your typical inventory where you make a list of everything. This will be a chart or list of the activities and needs you have in each area of your home and what you need to meet those needs. While this may sound simple or obvious, you will be surprised to find the items that fit or don't fit in a particular room.

Next, write down all the services to which you subscribe, including your telephone, utilities, cable television and online services. If you haven't already done so, get a calendar where you can record every activity, appointment and meeting that you have.

Once you write down every item, service and time commitment, you will find it easier to make a decision about what you really need.

Defining Your Needs

The theory put forth by Maslow in his *Hierarchy of Needs* says that 'people are motivated to fulfill basic needs before moving on to other more advanced needs'. In other words, we need to have our physiological needs, such as shelter, food, water, sleep and other basic requirements met before we can move on to other levels of need. We also have higher levels of need for safety and security, a feeling of belonging and love, self-esteem and self-actualization.

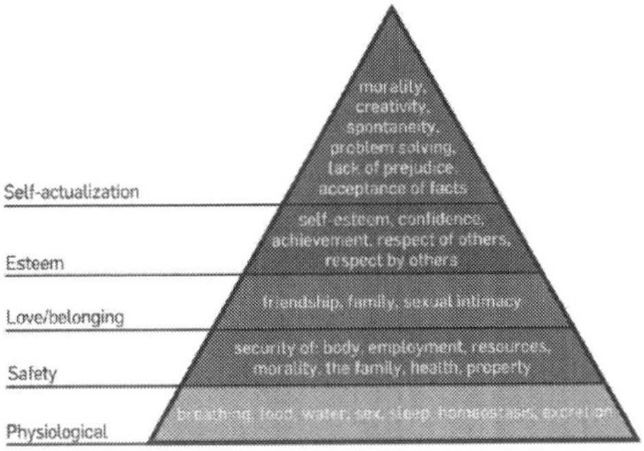

morality,
creativity,
spontaneity,
problem solving,
lack of prejudice
acceptance of facts
Self-actualization
self-esteem, confidence,
achievement, respect of others,
respect by others
Esteem
friendship, family, sexual intimacy
Love/belonging
security of: body, employment, resources,
morality, the family, health, property
Safety
Physiological

Living simply is not about discarding your basic necessities. You need to have these things so you can move on to increasing levels of contentment and satisfaction. Unfortunately once we have met these needs, we can find ourselves on an incredible pace of accumulating more and more things that we tell ourselves will make us happy and bring a higher level of esteem. Until now, when you have begun the process to reevaluate your belongings and lifestyle.

If you were to lose everything, where would you start? What would be you first goal to accomplish and why? Several years ago, an interview with an American hostage revealed that a lack of toilet paper made him feel extreme levels of anxiety. Obviously, living without certain necessary items opposes the basic philosophy of minimalism.

If you want to live your life as a minimalist, do not discard the necessities that help you live a healthy and harmonious lifestyle. Keep items that cause you to experience a strong mind and healthy body.

Once we reach this stage, we can now begin to tackle specific items analyze how these things fit into over overall needs, wants and desire for simplicity.

CHAPTER 8

THE IF-THEN MODEL

Now that you have defined your overall goal of what is important and necessary to you, we will work on fitting each and every item, service and time zapper into that definition. Here are some questions you can ask yourself as you organize your items and eliminate some.

- Is this item here because I haven't made a decision where it belongs?
- Do I really treasure and appreciate this item?
- If I were shopping today, is this something I would buy?
- Will I be able to wear this dress, pants, or pair of shoes again…ever?
- If this item were broken, would I pay to get it fixed?
- Do I even own the main gadget that this part belongs to?
- Does this item add to my stress level?
- Is this thing necessary to reduce stress?

- Will this help me to have some extra time?
- Does this item cause me extra work or time?
- Is this just taking up space or do I really like it?
- Does this thing make me happy?
- Is this item really meaningful to me?
- Am I keeping this item out of a sense of loss or guilt?
- Is it necessary for me to work on the weekends?
- Do I need 400+ cable channels or can I do with less? Or none?
- Is there an alternate service, i.e. phone, internet, cable, that would cost me less money?
- Do I really use that membership enough that it justifies the cost?

As you may have noticed, many of these questions start with an IF statement or a close variation. A common rule in decision theory goes like this; If this statement is true, then do this. If this statement is false, then do this. We frequently find ourselves with excess clutter or disorganization because we haven't asked the right questions.

Try this exercise to see what I mean. Pick up an item in your house and ask yourself one of these questions. Depending upon your answer, the item will be placed back where it was, put into a storage container or area, thrown out, or donated.

1. If I saw this vase today in a store, would I purchase it? If yes, keep it or store it. If no, get rid of it. If you keep it, ask the next question. If I really want to keep this, would I put it in its same spot? Somewhere

else? Or put it in a storage container to be used later.

2. Is this pile of mail here because I don't know what to do with it or don't want to deal it right now? You need to set up a system; junk out the door and important items filed. The filed items need to have a meaningful file name, e.g. insurance documents, bills to pay – in time-sensitive files, or catalogues to read and then throw out.

Don't want to do it right now? Get past this feeling...because it only gets worse later. Quickly dispose of this mail task and you won't even know it happened. Minutes of your time lead to a lot less clutter and wasted time.

3. If you work so many hours every week that you don't have enough time to participate in activities outside of work or are too exhausted too, then you need to evaluate what you are doing with your time and determine if these activities are really necessary and add value to your life.

- Are you working on weekends or late into the evening?
- Could you be more productive and use your time more efficiently during the week.
- Could you delegate more of your work?
- Is everything you do adding value or could you just eliminate some things without any consequences?

If you do have to work, can you just set aside a period of time on Sunday evening to tackle your work? This way you won't have scattered your work throughout your weekend and ruined your time to regroup and refresh. Plus you will be all ready to get for Monday morning and it will be fresh in your mind.

As you can see the IF-THEN Model requires asking yourself a question about your possessions or activities. Then, based upon your answer, you will take one of two courses of action. Follow the diagram below to make the steps easier. At the 'decision' diamond, if your item or activity fits your definition of necessary, then you follow the diagram to the left and you are finished. If you find that your answer to the necessity question is 'no' then you must go through the 'gears' to do something about that before you can complete the process.

As you can see by the diagram, there is no room for a 'maybe'. Every item you assess must have a defined outcome.

There are many other questions and even more *variations* of these questions that you will be honestly answering about each one of the things that are cluttering your life and causing stress. You may find yourself digging deeper to answer a question about some items. By using the If-Then Model you will simplify your process and ensure you get satisfactory results.

PART THREE

GETTING IT DONE

> I am always doing that which I can not do, in order that I may learn how to do it.
> — Pablo Picasso

CHAPTER 9

DECLUTTER AND TAKE CONTROL

Now that I have laid the foundation and you know how to get yourself in the right mindset, it's time to get down to business. I would bet by now you are chomping at the bit and are ready to go. You have the tools that will help you throughout this process.

Let's start by giving you several of my top tricks and tips for getting your space under control. These will give you some more ideas on how to prepare yourself for organizing and simplifying. Next we will get into many of the quick and easy tricks that will help you see immediate results. And Results = Motivation so these tools will get you going and keep you going.

Top tips for decluttering your living space:

Take baby steps. It could be a baby kitten or a baby elephant. My advice is to start small enough that you can get it done in 20 minutes or can declutter one item - a shelf, a drawer, a counter top. Then attack another area the next day. If you decide to tackle an entire room or closet or chest, you can easily get overwhelmed.

When we feel overwhelmed, it becomes way too easy to procrastinate and leave it for another day - which may never ever come. You could also get interrupted if your task takes too long, leaving you with whatever you were cleaning out now wide out in the open - clearly not what we were trying to accomplish. So start small and see some progress. There is nothing like a small victory to keep up motivated!

Set aside 20 minutes - or your estimated time to accomplish your one item on your schedule - **every day**. Put it on your calendar just like you would write down a dental appointment. Alright - it's really not that painful... Depending upon my day and motivation level, I might set aside more time. This is because I either have some extra time or I am utterly and completely motivated to tackle a particular area. I take care of this area either small or big and get it all done. The feeling of accomplishment is amazing! Once you start to see the progress and the benefits it almost becomes addicting.

Set up your boundaries. Focus on one item or small area at a time - shelf, drawer, counter top. Alternatively, if you have set aside your 20 minutes, stick to that time limit. Then do that one item or area completely, or fully use the time you set aside. It is ideal if you can plan the area or project to fit your allotted time.

Have a trash bag, donation box, storage container and your definition of necessity ready to go. Completely empty out the space you have designated to work on today. Next, sort through each item. Many items will be easy to deal with. You will know immediately if it can be thrown in the trash or donated. Take care of those items immediately. Then you will be left with the in-between items. Some of these items you will 'think' you may need some day. Other items may have a sentimental value. Still other items you may use, but haven't don't so in a very long time.

Think about your definition of necessity. Better yet, have a piece of paper with your definition written down and taped to the wall right next to you. Now make a choice. Handle the item once. Don't put it in a 'maybe' pile and re-handle it again. Doing so only takes time and makes the decision even harder. Wipe out the area you have just emptied and only put back the items you need to keep. Notice I said 'need' to...

Be ruthless. By ruthless I don't mean following some arbitrary rule that says if it's over a year old, toss it. Frankly, I think that 'rule' is ridiculous and also makes it very hard for us to embrace simplicity. In some ways that rule seems counter-intuitive to me. Heck if I've had it over a year, there could be a chance I really like it or use it frequently.

I have a great stand mixer that I received from my mother who got it as a wedding gift in 1945. That stand mixer is one of the tools I use in my kitchen frequently. Better yet, that mixer has outlasted many other small kitchen appliances I have purchased in the last decade. I am sure you can relate to this – how often have you purchased something and it totally dies in a year or less, with no service that will fix it and it they do it's easier or cheaper to replace the gadget.

However, you should be honest with yourself. If you haven't used it for a long time, get rid of it. If it's a part of something else you no longer own, get rid of it. If it's just 'cute' or has a minor sentimental value, get rid of it. Be reasonable and thoughtful about the stuff you throw out or give away. If it's really not useful or is in terrible condition, just throw it out and don't pass junk off to a donation center.

Get Ready for the Domino Effect. I am sure you know the feeling. Have you ever painted your living room walls and suddenly the dining room or foyer looks a bit dingy? Have you ever bought a new washer and not a new dryer? I didn't think so. Well the same holds true with reducing your clutter. Clean off one shelf and suddenly the others look dreadful. Clean out one drawer and you will get remarkably frustrated with how hard it is to find something in the others. That cluttered counter top? It suddenly sticks out like a sore thumb.

There is nothing like the good feelings from getting rid of the junk and having something clean and organized. It's rejuvenating! When you experience that, the motivation to take on the next shelf or drawer or larger area becomes a reality. Step back and enjoy what you have started!

Be realistic. Or maybe by this time you are telling *me* to 'get real'. Telling yourself you can sort and depart with many of these items you have collected for such a long time and that now, finally that by some miracle, you will be able to make that choice may seem unrealistic.

So, if you must, start another storage box with the 'maybe' and the 'omg I just can't' get rid of items'. But please put them all in another storage area. Don't leave the onesies and twosies cluttered amongst all your other items. If you do you will have to re-sort them at another time and they will still be cluttering up you vital space. Put that box out of site.

So now you have this 'other' must keep item box. Wait six months or a year. Take out that box and reevaluate the contents. Go through the same steps that I listed above. If the item still is important - keep it. If not - toss. Sooner or later, these extraneously items will get taken care of.

Don't recreate your problem. Once you have that drawer, shelf or other area cleaned out, don't add items to it. Or if you really, really must add something, take something away. Follow the same steps you have used to clean it out before - decide if it is necessary and if not, toss it or donate it. Always keep in mind how good it felt and feels to keep it organized. Don't give up on your goals. Create a system and a mindset that you can always use so you don't start piling stuff up again.

Celebrate your accomplishments! Step back and enjoy the new look! Even if it is small, recognize that it is a start - a big start. Make a note on your calendar. Cross it off your to-do list. Even that simple task feels amazing. It's a great start. Pat yourself on the back. Pause a moment.

Treat yourself to something. Give yourself a simple reward - possibly one that resides in your definition of what's important to you. Take a breath. Plan the next activity.

CHAPTER 10

QUICK START DECLUTTERING

The main idea with this section is to help you get some quick results so that you feel like you have accomplished something. The sooner you can do that the better and better this process will feel. Plus it does get rid of much of the basic clutter. Worst case scenario is that if you don't do anything more after this, you will still have accomplished a lot.

Also called *Easy In Easy Out,* these steps will help you get the items out of your door that you don't have to make hard decisions about. The came in easy, they go out easy. Once you have this done it will be easier for you to get down to the nitty gritty of cleaning and organizing your spaces.

Garbage Bag Spree

This is similar to the shopping spree contests that are run for fun. The contestants are given a shopping cart and have 30 seconds to get all the items they want in to their cart. Whoever has the highest total value items receives the groceries in their cart for free.

For our purposes, the garbage bag spree involves…you guessed it, a garbage bag and 5 minutes to race through a room and collect all of the junk that you know you can and should throw away. This 'game' turns what is a dreaded chore into a fun game. Additionally, this is a great way to get kids and family members engaged in cleaning your rooms and tidying things up. Make it into a contest and offer a simple prize – an extra 15 minutes of TV, a back massage or a night off from loading the dishwasher.

Every Item In Its Place

When you are done with the garbage bag spree, run another game to find all of the items that aren't in their right 'home' and put them back. This game is only for items that are sitting out on the surface that you can quickly make a decision about. For example, this includes things like a dirty glass that was left on the coffee table, the remote control that is in-between the cushions on the sofa or the car keys that got tossed on the kitchen cupboard.

Recycle Old Newspapers

If you subscribe to the local newspaper seven days a week, you may find it tempting to keep them in several neat piles. Besides the possibility of causing a fire, piles of newspapers are unsightly and serve to make a room look completely cluttered. You may think you need all those old newspapers for future reference, but you can always look up past news articles online. As long as you resist the temptation to print everything you read on your printer, you will have eliminated clutter that also poses a safety hazard in your home.

Buy Airtight Plastic Storage Bags

Closet space is always a challenge. If you still possess a large wardrobe, and you have a small bedroom closet, buy large airtight plastic storage bags in which you can store clothes. Store winter clothes, hats, scarves and mittens in storage bags during the warmer months of the year, and store your shorts and summer tops in sealed bags during the colder seasons.

Airtight bags hold a large amount of clothes while taking up a small amount of space. You can pile the airtight bags in a neat row without creating a cluttered closed. Additionally, you may want to buy a shoe rack for storing your shoes and keeping them off the floors. A great shoe bag is one that can hang behind a door. I have one that can hold 24 pairs of shoes or other items. The best part about this is that it uses space on the back side of a door that isn't being used for anything else and you gets items off the floor and into an easily accessible spot.

How to Throw out your Garbage

You may think that throwing out garbage is a mindless task, but, if you go about it the right way, you can eliminate excessive clutter in your home. Before you take a bag of garbage out, check your refrigerator, kitchen cupboards, closets, bathroom and floors. Throw out any suspicious items that tell you they are nothing more than possessions that will eventually clutter up your house. It is easy to save newspapers, soap shavings and empty shampoo bottles. You save stuff because you have convinced yourself that you will find uses for them in the future.

If you actually have a reason to save something, then the item is not constituted under the clutter category. The best thing is to throw out questionable items because if you allow them to pile up in every room, your house is going to have a cluttered atmosphere within a short amount of time. Just throwing out one additional item every time you take out the garbage will start to reduce your clutter substantially.

Keep Clutter off your Floors

One simple way to prevent clutter is to get out of the habit of tossing clothes, toys, books and games on floors. When pressed for time, throwing items on the floor seems like a practical solution, but you will only succeed in creating an unbelievable amount of clutter within a few days or a week. Always throw your dirty clothes in the laundry or put them back in your closet or drawer where they belong. Buy a few magazine racks for storing magazines, newspapers and weekly grocery store flyers. Buy a few toy chests, and instruct your children to put their toys, games and dolls in the toy chests whenever they are finished playing.

Eliminate Free Plastic Shopping Bags

If you are like most people, you probably save your free plastic shopping bags whenever you bring groceries into your home. Fill up one large plastic bag with other bags. When one designated bag is full, throw out the excess plastic bags. You do not need to own a thousand plastic bags that soon take up an excessive amount of space in your kitchen pantry or closet.

Do not Collect Junk Mail and Expired Coupons

If you receive a lot of junk mail, do not turn worthless letters into a hobby. Instead, get into the habit of throwing out junk mail as soon as you receive it. Take a quick glance to make sure it really is a piece of junk mail, and then throw it in a plastic garbage bag. Throw your junk mail bags into your trash bin every week. Keep other letters and documents you receive in the mail, such as bank statements and mutual fund confirmations, in special boxes, containers or file cabinets.

If you save coupons, put them in an easily accessible folder. When you find new coupons, remove the expired coupons form the folder before you add the new ones. If you can look for coupons online for your favorite items or download an app to you phone that will get you great savings but won't create physical clutter.

CHAPTER 11

DIGGING DEEPER

By now you should be feeling pretty good about the progress you have made. You should see a huge improvement over your previous surroundings. Now it's time to dig a little deeper and use the skills we learned to simplify our life even more.

Plan One Day at a Time

Organizing your house is a challenging task, but if you plan to organize the items you keep one day at a time, you will not experience an excessive amount of stress. In order to accomplish this task, break down your inventory list into sub-categories.

For example, you may want to organize your clothes as the first step in your organizing plan. If so, make a separate list and call it List Number One. Work on organizing your clothes first, and do not plan on organizing any other items on your list until you have accomplished this task. Every item in your inventory list needs to fall under specific categories, and each category should have its own time frame.

Take a Good Look at your Possessions

If your closets contain bags filled with stuff, you need to empty each bag and look at the contents. Put items that do not serve any useful purposes in separate piles. If a pile contains useless antiques, consider selling them or giving them to a relative or close friend. While you may not find any value in these antiques, another person may treasure them. If you really need to hold on to an item, then again it is probably not clutter.

How to Categorize Clutter

You may have purchased an item for a low price at a garage sale, thinking that you will use it one day. However, you bought the garage sale item five years ago, and it has resided in your closet all this time. Perhaps you own clothes that used to fit before you gained 25 pounds. Your kids may own toys and dolls they used to play with when they were toddlers. If you still hold onto socks that lack their mates, just get rid of them and buy some brand new socks if you do have a need for more.

Any item you own that you do not use is an item you do not need, unless it serves to promote happiness and harmony in your home. Items you may use occasionally, such as needles and threads or bandages, are not useless because they have the potential to serve valuable purposes from time to time. If you own a pair of shoes you purchased when you visited Paris, it is time to start wearing them once in a while. Find a dress-up event to attend, and wear your designer shoes instead of burying them in your closet.

How to Part with Gifts

If you are similar to most people, you probably own several gifts you received for birthday or Christmas presents. While gifts often have sentimental value, they can create clutter. If you want to evaluate a lack of organization in your home, you need to examine the many gifts you have received from well-meaning friends or loved ones. You may use some of these gifts all the time, but other presents remain in hiding somewhere in a nook or cranny of your closet or dresser drawer.

Every item you eliminate means one less piece of clutter, so analyze the gifts you own to ascertain whether you really need or want to keep them as mementos, or whether you need to relegate them into one of your junk piles. Remember that an organized household is supposed to cause you to feel better about your lifestyle. If donating or tossing a specific gift causes you to feel sad or anxious, then keep the item, and regard it as a necessary possession.

Do not Keep Items Because of Guilty Feelings

Guilt is not a pleasant emotion. You may feel guilty about many things in your life, but harboring guilty feelings about getting rid of old watches with broken wristbands or hand-me-down rings with missing gemstones will not help you evaluate the clutter in your life in the correct way. You may have inherited your deceased aunt's collection of unattractive antique glassware, but you continue to keep the glasses because of guilty feelings. Instead of feeling guilty, give the glasses to another person or charitable organization. Someone will then actually enjoy drinking their favorite beverages from your aunt's glasses, which means that you have transformed your clutter into something of value.

Learn How to Let Go of Items you no Longer Need

During your evaluation process, you are bound to feel mixed emotions while trying to decide whether to keep or eliminate items. Even though letting go of unused items may cause some stress in the beginning, you may feel a sense of relief once you realize that your home is more organized. Look at the objects you own in a realistic way, without attaching yourself to each item. Letting go is not easy, but if you do not learn how to let go of some items, your home will still lack organization.

Books, Music and Movie Collections

If you collect CDs, books and videos, your entire collection is not necessarily clutter. You need to evaluate each item as an individual entity. If you play music every night, and read your books whenever you have the chance, your collection is not clutter. Remember that clutter does not generally promote feelings of happiness. If your collection makes you feel happy, the CDs, books and movies you own are necessary items because they create harmony.

Artwork

Similarly, original signed paintings by well-known artists are only clutter if they make you feel sad. Your walls should only contain artwork that inspires you. Eliminate drawings or paintings that cause you to feel depressed or that create a gloomy atmosphere in your home. Cheerful images can help you create a positive ambiance in your living room or bedroom. Any work of art that causes depression or anxiety, no matter how costly, is part of your clutter collection.

You may also want to look at items that you once loved but no longer fits your tastes. Sometimes we buy artwork and don't display it right away. If you have items like this, the best idea is to sell them or give them away since they are not adding to your happiness.

Getting rid of artwork is always a difficult task for me. After all, I typically paid good money for the items and very much enjoyed the purchase. The difficult thing about art is that it causes emotional reactions in us. However if these items are sitting in a closet they are no longer giving you the emotional high that you thought would happen. What you need to do to make a decision about artwork is ask yourself if the piece still generates a strong positive emotional reaction in yourself. Does it do this to the extent that it is worth keeping? Does the good feeling you get from a particular piece outweigh the happiness you get from simplifying?

Your Clutter is Another Person's Prized Possession

Host a Huge Yard Sale Event. Hosting a yard sale is a simple way to get rid of stuff you no longer need. Check to see if you can find newspapers offering free classified advertisements for yard sales. Drive around your neighborhood to find stores, community centers and other buildings with bulletin boards. People can only go to so many yard sales in one day, so positive mental images of your sale needs to stand out in their minds and appeal to their emotions.

List Items On eBay or Craigslist. These are great places to sell items and work especially well for the larger ticket items. You should also use these if you just don't want to or can't host a yard sale.

Remember that just because you decided that your depressing painting is nothing but clutter, another person may view it in a different light. You see, the people who want to buy your stuff are most likely individuals who still live in homes containing clutter. Yes, yard sale customers collect the type of clutter you are now eliminating. The clutter cycle continues from your yard to another person's house.

CHAPTER 12

TRANSITION TIME

Getting organized is more than selling items in a yard sale and placing your remaining possessions in labeled plastic bags, in drawers and on shelves. You also need to make sure that the system you have created works well with your daily routine.

If you feel like you have done a great job going over your items and removing anything unnecessary you can skip this next step or save it for a later date.

Go Through Your Stuff One More Time

Now that you have sold and donated the items you previously evaluated as constituting clutter, go through your closets, dressers, drawers and shelves a second time. Your mind now sees things more clearly, and you will find it easier to evaluate other items you no longer need to own.

When you first looked at all your stuff, you may have felt overwhelmed with the idea of eliminating so many items. Perhaps you had serious doubts about eliminating some valuables. These objects are still residing in your relatively uncluttered house. Since you are now used to the idea of eliminating clutter, you will find it easier to sort through other doubtful possessions and create a few more piles of unnecessary stuff.

Organize the Items you Plan to Keep

After you sell or donate the items you no longer need to own, you need to organize the items you plan to keep. Separate your items into specific categories and sub-categories. If you have a pile of antiques, separate jewelry from paintings. Organize books you plan to keep according to subject matter. Put classic novels in one pile, contemporary novels in a second pile, poetry books in a third pile and biographies in a fourth pile.

Organize your CDs according to musician and band names. Divide clothes into piles consisting of dress clothes, casual outfits, dress shoes, athletic shoes, hats and other accessories. Make separate piles of clothes and accessories for young boys and girls, teenage boys, teenage girls, adult males and adult females.

Use Your Activities Inventory to Begin Organizing

You will need this list now that it is time to organize your kept items in a way that makes sense. Before you eliminated items, you may have stored everything in your bedroom closet. Now, it is time to store items in their proper places. Get them out of the closet and into their proper spaces. When you see your books, CDs, pots and pans in full view, or at least on shelves in appropriate rooms, you will use them. Otherwise, the items you decided to keep during your evaluation process will only amount to more clutter.

Make a Plan to Add Additional Storage Space in your Kitchen

You do not need to have your kitchen remodeled to create additional space. You can buy one or two utility carts for storing extra pots, pans, dishes, glasses and silverware. Utility carts also hold plates and bowls, and you can wheel the carts into your dining room to use when serving dinner guests.

There are so many ways that you can free up space in your kitchen just by storing items in unused spaces such as behind cupboard doors, below your top cupboards or from the ceiling such as a pot rack or wine holder.

Embrace the Changes You See

By this stage, you should see enormous changes to your environment. Keep in mind that you won't accomplish everything overnight. Decluttering, organizing and simplifying are an ongoing process with enormous benefits. Take time to reflect on what you have already accomplished and enjoy the benefits of minimalism.

Do not Accumulate Items that Lead to Clutter

The reason you accumulated clutter in the past is because you allowed items to pile up until they were out of control. Your possessions can seem to take on a mind of their own if they get out of hand. Pretty soon, you can almost hear them speak to you as though they are characters in an animated film.

Remember that items you do not need do not serve any useful purposes, and they prevent you from sticking to your original plan about keeping clutter under control. One way to master your urge to collect useless items is to make throwing out the trash a work of art.

Buy Affordable Bookshelves, Hangers, Shoe Racks and Hampers

If you are a bibliophile, buy a few bookshelves, and place them in the room where you read books. You can find inexpensive bookshelves at thrift stores and garage sales, or you can build your own shelves.

You already know that your clothes belong either in the bedroom closet or in a hamper. If you are constantly adding clothes to your wardrobe, keep plenty of hangers on hand. Buy some hangers with clasps for hanging up pants and skirts. Buy a few shoe racks for storing dress shoes, athletic shoes and slippers, and keep a shoe rack in every bedroom closet.

Keep a hamper in each bathroom or bedroom so family members have places in which to toss their dirty clothes and towels. Then, do your laundry on a regular basis.

Decorative Cardboard Boxes

You can get inexpensive, sturdy, colorful boxes at craft and discount stores for storing useful items you may want to keep. You can use these boxes to store photos, CDs, DVDs, pens, pencils, paper clips and notepads. Label each box. When you are finished labeling your boxes, arrange them on a section of a closet shelf or a bookshelf.

Check your Home Several Days a Week

One thing to remember about clutter is that it multiplies quickly, so it is helpful to check every room, closet and cupboard for clutter on a regular basis. You may be following all the recommended steps for putting everything in its place immediately, but items still can pile up. You may have gotten interrupted, or just took 'fell off the wagon', or the *clutter gremlins* could have snuck in things while you weren't looking.

Whatever the reason, you will find that you need to make a quick run through the house and take care of some items. However, this should be a very quick and easy task now that you have eliminated so much excess. Doing this every day or once a week will help you to keep yourself organized and clutter free.

Eliminate older clothes whenever you buy new clothes. Get rid of your favorite pair of worn out shoes with holes in the toes, and replace them with new shoes. When you live an uncluttered lifestyle, you create a home with a harmonious and peaceful atmosphere.

Organize Your Mornings

For instance, if you always get ready for work at the last minute, place your favorite cereal boxes within easy reach rather than keeping them at the back of your cupboard shelf. Keep sugar in a lidded sugar bowl in easy reach so you do not need to open a bag stored on your shelf every time you want to sweeten your morning cup of coffee. Simple strategies save you time and give you a sense of organization.

PART FOUR

FUNCTIONAL SPACES

> "All life is an experiment.
> The more experiments
> you make the better.
> - Ralph Waldo Emerson

CHAPTER 13

COMMON LIVING AREAS

One area that I like to encourage people to start with is the living room, family room and dining room. These rooms are where everyone in the household can see and feel the benefits of decluttering and simplifying. These are also the rooms typically seen first by visitors and will create their first impression.

While this may sound obvious, by definition a living room is for living; not a place to drop your stuff when you get in the door, not a dining room and most certainly not a storage room. The goal here is to define how you want to functionally use this space. Do you watch TV here? Do your family and friends play games here? Do you like to read or do projects, such as knitting, in this space? Do children like to play here? However you want to use this space will help you declutter and organize the space so that it feels useful and stress free.

For your initial steps, I will go with the assumption that you have already done the 'garbage bag run' and the 'everything in its place' activities. In other words, disposables such as old papers, magazines or empty pizza boxes are gone and the oddball items such as dirty dishware and socks have found their rightful home. If you have done those tasks well, you are now able to tackle the bigger task of organizing and getting the space you really want so you can enjoy it.

1. Close your eyes and think about what your ideal space would look like. If you were to take everything out of that room, would everything make it back into your ideal space? Too often we keep furniture we don't use or doesn't help us use our space ideally just because we have always had it that way.

If an item that you 'took' out of your imagined room wouldn't make it back in to your ideal room, then remove it. Either sell it, donate it or otherwise get rid of it. If you aren't sure at first, temporarily move the item into a storage area. After a month if you don't miss the item, get rid of it. Chances are you won't miss it at all. Or possibly you have re-purposed it into another room – just remember it needs to serve a purpose – not just get moved somewhere else because we aren't sure how to part with it.

2. Keep an open mind about what 'belongs' in your room. Just because a coffee table is a 'typical' item to own and all the furniture show rooms display living areas with them, it doesn't mean they are ideal for you.

When my daughter was a toddler, we removed our coffee table from the living room. I was amazed at how such a simple thing opened up my space and made it feel much larger – also much less to clean. It also gave us more open space to play in the center of activity, especially for an active child, but also eliminated some unnecessary bumped noggins and stubbed toes.

When I shared this simple, yet effective, idea with a colleague of mine, she adopted the idea so that now she can now do yoga in that space. Remember it is all about what works functionally and simply for you.

3. Check if there are items that really don't belong there. This process can apply to furniture items or any other miscellany. If you look at your entertainment center or cabinets, do you have entertaining, valuable and useful items in them or have they become collection spots for 'stuff' you don't know where to put anywhere else or haven't put in their rightful home. You don't do laundry in the living room so it also isn't a place to pile unfolded or dirty clothes…sounds strange, but I've seen this more times than I should.

If you have a collection of porcelain figurines, trophies or framed pictures that you enjoy looking at and taking center stage in your room, then by all means keep them there. They make take up space and take time to dust, but if they give you pleasure then they deserve a rightful spot in your room.

4. Don't acquire things unnecessarily that you have nowhere to put them unless you plan to eliminate something else. This also applies to

COMMON LIVING AREAS | 79

buying furniture or electronics that are oversized for your space. Your space won't expand, it will only make the space you already have seem much smaller.

A rather unusual example of this came to me when picking up my daughter at a schoolmates house several years ago. As I went from the foyer past the formal dining room, I noticed large cages sitting on the dining room table. As it turns out, this was the home of the children's pet hamsters. If you are trying to achieve minimalism and you don't have a realistic place for any item, including pets, just don't buy them until you do or don't acquire them at all.

Potentially this family may have decided that they don't need a dining room – they may have a large eat-in area in the kitchen that works very well for them – and therefore decided to use the dining space as something else. This would be fine, since it follows the my suggested practice of determining what makes you happy and using your space accordingly. However, if that is the case, then I would highly suggest converting the space to its new functional purpose. If you want an extra play room or to house your pet hamsters, then rework the space to satisfy that purpose. The pseudo dining room – pet room concept does not constitute functional, stress-free design.

Whether right or wrong, this observation immediately created an impression in my mind about the people who lived there. Think about what your living space says about you. Early on, work on simplifying areas that you use the most and are accessible to guests. This isn't to say that you should design your rooms to please others. However, there is a high probability that if you simplify your living areas to your desires, they will be pleasing to visitors.

Nothing creates a more stress-free, welcoming environment than clean and open spaces.

CHAPTER 14

KITCHENS AND PANTRY

When the kitchen is organized and aesthetically pleasing, the space works efficiently and it is a pleasure to spend time in the room.

The Basics

One of the first things you should do and will continue to do is to check for outdated items in your refrigerator or pantry. There are most likely a few items lurking there, so just get rid of them and the remainder of your space will suddenly get more manageable.

Clear everything off of the countertop. Thoroughly clean and disinfect the countertops, stove top and top of the refrigerator. If there are items such as mail or keys that don't belong in there move them to their appropriate space in the house. You can now replace items such as a coffee pot or utensil holder that you use frequently and fits the needs of this area. Don't put back any other items that don't fit this description.

Practical Organizing

Every kitchen has a different configuration, but there is a bottom line common sense theme as to where everything should be stored.

My first rule is that everything should be kept as close to where it is used as possible, and that the most often used items should be the most easily accessible.

Organizing an entire room can feel daunting, so I prefer to tackle the project in small steps. Whether you approach kitchen organization as one big overhaul, or in phases, the ultimate goal is to create an efficient working space that is easy to maintain.

Silverware, Utensils and Knives

Silverware usually occupies a top drawer, preferably near the dishwasher. There are many options for drawer inserts to hold flatware including hardwood, bamboo, plastic and open coated wire. They also come in many different sizes, so to get the best fit, measure the length, width and depth of the drawer. You may want to combine more than one to make the most of the drawer space.

There are a few options for storing cooking utensils. If you have drawer space, then drawer inserts or dividers will accommodate most. I prefer to have utensils near the stove, and store them in a stainless holder. The container is an opportunity to add color and interest on the counter or stove. Another option is to install a rack with hooks or just any kind of hooks on the wall to hang larger cooking utensils. I always look at kitchen wall space as potential storage.

Knives can be kept in knife holders made for drawers or attractive wood blocks for above counter storage. You may want more than one block to hold utility knives and steak knives. There are other choices including magnetic bars and blocks that can be mounted on the wall.

Everyday Dinnerware and Drinking Glasses

It is most convenient to store plates, bowls and often used serving dishes near the dishwasher. Glassware is more flexible and having it near the refrigerator may feel easier. If you have glass cabinets, you may want to store your most attractive items in those as long as they are organized and you use this idea sparingly.

Pots and Pans

I am a big advocate of hanging pots and pans. There are so many pot racks out there, in every style and form. They can hang from a pot rack directly from the ceiling, corner mounted, or even just hooks on a wall. I hate getting on my hands and knees to retrieve pots from bottom cabinets. Installing a pot rack is the one change I made in my kitchen that made the biggest difference and I like the look. If you must store your pots and pans in cabinets, it really helps to get pullouts and/or dividers. Lids can be stored with vertical dividers in a cabinet or deep drawer.

Bakeware, Mixing Bowls and Cutting Boards

Baking pans and bowls of all sizes can usually be stacked in a cabinet near the stove. Cookie sheets and cutting boards are best stored vertically. That makes them easy to see and use. There are many cabinet dividers to accommodate vertical storage, or you may have a narrow cabinet that works very well for them.

Spices, Cooking Oils and Other Cooking Essentials

Spices offer countless options when it comes to storage. There are many attractive spice racks at every price point. In my kitchen, we have a maple wood one on the counter and a metal one on the shelf above the stove. The items that are out in the open are the ones that I use almost daily.

I love to cook so I have a large collection of spices and various seasonings. I utilize a stair-step-holder in the cupboard for these items so that I can easily see them all. I also have them alphabetized. This makes it easy to find one item in a large collection and also is easy to see if you are out of an item. I initially did this project as a game to practice the alphabet with my preschool child. Today I still use this system and have so for years and absolutely love it.

You may have space to add narrow shelves or get a wall mounted holder to store spices above the stove or on a nearby wall. I am a fan of matching glass bottles to hold spices. It is a fun project to fill the glass bottles and label the ones that are displayed.

Another great trick is to put your spices in glass container with a metal top. Place a magnetic strip on the wall or under the cabinets and you attach your spice jars to the magnet. This design frees up space, makes your items accessible and can be very decorative.

Oils and other bottles, pepper grinders and salt can be kept in an adjacent cabinet, on a shelf, or in a tray or basket on or near the range. All of these cooking essentials can also be on a lazy-susan in an easy to reach cabinet.

Pantry Items

Organize your pantry items by category or cuisine. For example, pasta and sauce items, Chinese food, Mexican food, and soups should each be grouped in their own area. This system makes it much easier to quickly put together your meal when you are cooking. It also helps you to easily see if you have all of the ingredients you need without digging through the cupboards. I also find that by organizing this way, I don't have any expired items in my pantry and don't buy unnecessary items or duplicates at the grocery store.

Coffee and Wine Stations

Most kitchens have a coffee maker on the counter. The only thing I will say is that it helps to keep the coffee and supplies within easy reach of the pot. There are many pod holders available for the single cup brewers, or you can fill a colorful bowl with pods. If you are short on cabinet space, you can hang coffee mugs under a cabinet near the maker.

Wine storage is incorporated into most kitchens these days. There is every kind of wine bottle holder/rack. They can serve as utility and art. A wine rack can be free standing, mounted on the wall, under cabinet…use your imagination. It is easy, convenient and attractive to hang wine glasses under a cabinet, or to display them in a glass cabinet. Another option is to use a nice tray and keep wine and glasses on the counter.

Cookbooks and Family Recipes

If you love cookbooks and cooking magazines, chances are you have accumulated droves of them over the years. One of the harder things to part with in the kitchen, at least for me, is a cookbook. However, you really need to look at the cookbook itself and decide if you really do use it enough, if at all. If you use it frequently, then by all means keep it and put it in a handy spot – preferably a bookshelf – either in the kitchen or in close proximity.

If you really haven't used any recipe from the cookbook or food magazine, there is a good chance you won't *ever* use a recipe from it. Donate it, drop if off at your local library or just throw it out. Someone will benefit from this book more than you will.

A friend's mother once told me that if she can find one good recipe from a cookbook, then it is worth the purchase. I tend to agree. Plus this also helped me 'justify' an abundance of cookbook purchases. However, one recipe does not justify two to three inches of shelf space. Just take a copy of the recipe, put it in a recipe binder or recipe box and get rid of the whole book. Not only do you reduce your clutter and gain more space, but the recipe is now much easier to find and is a good time saver.

There are so many functional and fun recipe binders that you can find in gift and card shops, or even in a scrapbooking store, that you will appreciate your recipe collection even more.

Utility Items – The Infamous Junk Drawer

It is kind of a luxury to have hidden, pull out trash/recycle containers, but a decent sized stainless or colored flip top canister will also do the job. You don't have to look at the trash and a foot pedal to open makes for hands free, mess free disposal.

Again, pull outs are ideal for all the cleaners etc. stored under the sink, but any caddy or plastic bin will keep supplies contained.

A "junk" drawer is kind of a kitchen essential – because it holds pens, rubber bands, scissors, tape ... Flatware type inserts are all it takes to reign in the miscellaneous.

Kitchen "Art"

A completely "clutter" free kitchen feels sterile and uninviting. There are many opportunities to add color and interest combined with usefulness. Stand mixers are a staple and come in a rainbow of colors. I also keep an often used red cast iron Dutch Oven on my range top.

Other ways to incorporate useful art are hand towels and pot holders on hooks, beautiful pepper grinder, butter dish, salt and pepper shakers, and a tablecloth, just to name a few.

Organizing your kitchen reduces your time to make meals and makes the whole process inviting and relaxing. A kitchen that looks lived in and loved feels warm and inviting.

CHAPTER 15

BATHROOMS

The bathroom is probably the hardest working room in the house. And for most of us, it is the smallest room in our home. Given this, organization is even more important.

Eliminate the Samples and End of Life Items

How often do you receive samples from cosmetic counters and gifts for your purchase? Actually the more important question is, how often do you really use them, if ever. If you have never used them, including the cute little bag they came in, just throw them away. These items take up an enormous amount of space to say nothing of the fact that their shelf-life is limited. You do not need them and you certainly don't need them cluttering your bathroom or your precious storage.

Another frequent cause of clutter in the bathroom is almost finished tubes or containers. If you are using them currently, that's ok, if they are there because you want to remember the brand or you just didn't use it all up, then that item has got to go. Write down the brand name or special type and then toss the container.

Making Your Space Work

You should start with the overall feel of the space. The bathroom can be an opportunity to take risks with color – bright, soothing, clean colors – whatever color feels good. Then other elements can be coordinated with the color and the light. Natural light is great in any room, but not always plentiful in a bathroom.

One thing I have done in more than one bathroom, is to use a decorative, clear plastic shower curtain, rather than opaque. If the inside of your shower or bath has light colored tile, or is pleasant to look at, a clear shower curtain makes the space feel bigger and brighter overall. Personally, I always feel that a blue or a green (plant or color) element gives a bathroom a fresh, clean feel.

Vanity

The vanity is often the only, or the most space available to store everything. With drawers, inserts are essential. By measuring the length, width and depth, you can find containers that best fit. Plastic storage containers are cheap, and can be easily washed out once in a while. I also use plastic bins that are easy to pull in and out on the shelves inside the cabinets. You can store hair dryers, irons, combs, brushes in one, and products in another. Medicines are not really supposed to be stored in the bathroom, but if you do, a plastic bin with an airtight cover is a good choice.

The best thing for keeping cleaning supplies, etc. under the sink, is to get a roll out made for that space. There are also inside door mounts to hold bottles, shaving cream, and all the miscellaneous that ends up in the room. What ends up being stored on top of the vanity depends on the other space available. We will address multi use containers throughout this section.

Towel Racks and Hooks

Towel racks are fine, but if space is at a premium, hooks are best. They are not only an efficient way to keep towels and robes, but they can also double as art. And of course, the towels add texture, and if you choose, color to the room. Another option for hooks are over the door hangers. They are a great way to keep clothing and pajamas off the floor if the bathroom is also used as a changing room. If there is any way to squeeze in a hamper, that also helps to keep dirty clothes from being left in a pile on the floor. A coat rack is another idea for holding lots of stuff, while taking up minimal floor space.

Shelves

If you need extra space, the walls in a bathroom offer valuable real estate. An often ignored space is the wall above the toilet. There are many ready made over the toilet storage solutions, but even plain old shelves can add significant storage space. Most home stores have every kind and size of ready-made or custom cut wood for shelving. Again, this is an opportunity to add interest by using raw, painted or stained wood. You can use brackets or an invisible mount.

There may be room to add a narrow shelf between the sink or vanity top and the mirror above, especially if you are dealing with a pedestal sink. There are also surrounds made to go underneath pedestal sinks. If there is room, there are plenty of free standing shelving units in many sizes and shapes.

With any shelving solution, just make sure that you really need the items that are going to take up this shelving...and are willing and able to keep them clean. You only need this type of storage solution if you have totally paired down the items that you are keeping and the ones that need shelf space are indeed a necessity.

Bath and Shower Supplies

Of course, there are all kinds of products made that can hold everything we need to use in the shower. Just choose the ones you like and that best suit your needs. Here again, make sure these are items you really find necessary and use every day.

Last, But not Least ... Storage Containers

Once you have completed ridding your bathroom of unnecessary items, here is an opportunity to have fun with the organizing project. For larger items, or a whole collection of related products, I love to use baskets. Baskets come in every size, weave, color ... and add a textural element that is a great counterbalance to all of the shiny porcelain in the room.

Fabric and wooden totes are another good option. They can be color coded for different users. A round, colorful, silverware-type tote can hold toothbrushes and paste if they are not stashed in a drawer. Glass containers are perfect for cotton balls and Q-tips, and can be an attractive accessory on the vanity or a shelf.

Wire, woven, fabric and wood containers can add personality to the space while serving the function of holding rolled up towels and extra bathroom paper products.

My best suggestion to tackle a bathroom organization is to find a focal point that inspires you to be creative. It can be anything from wall color to beautiful towels to baskets to artful hooks ... use your imagination, and have fun!

CHAPTER 16

BEDROOMS

Having an organized bedroom can be amazingly beneficial to your overall wellness and happiness. It will help you sleep better, lower stress levels, make mornings easier, restore your energy and so much more. Unfortunately many of us do not have a nice, organized bedroom which we can relax in but instead find ourselves sleeping surrounded by clutter and mess.

On the bright side, it only takes a small amount of time and effort to get your bedroom organized and most importantly enjoyable. Follow the easy steps below and you will soon find yourself in a relaxing and accessible bedroom.

Laundry is for the Hamper not the Floor

It is very easy to let dirty clothes pile up all around your bedroom but in many cases this is the biggest source of clutter. Luckily this can be easily avoided by purchasing a hamper and developing the habit of using it. If clothes are dirty they should be put into the hamper instead of thrown into a pile or left scattered across the floor.

Once the hamper becomes full take it to the laundry room rather than letting it overflow onto the floor.

When the laundry comes back up from being washed, fold it and put it away. Don't let the pile of nice clean clothes sit until it is either worn or becomes dirty by just sitting there. These steps may seem like extra work but in the long run they will keep your bedroom much cleaner and more pleasant to be in.

Make Use of your Closet and Dresser.

One of the easiest ways to keep your bedroom clean and organized is by also keeping your clothes and shoes clean and organized. In the previous step we talked about how to keep the clothes in your bedroom clean but now let's talk about how to keep them organized too.

The absolutely best way to keep unclutter your bedroom is to put your clothes and shoes into your closet or dresser drawers immediately when you take them off or after having them laundered and cleaned. When changing outfits take an extra second to toss dirty items into the hamper or put them into your closet or drawers and you will be amazed how much cleaner your room will look.

However, the most important thing to remember when doing this is that wherever you put your clothes it must clutter free and organized. We will get in to more detail on this in the next Chapter on Organizing Your Closet.

By taking just a few minutes each time, you are removing objects from your room that cause clutter and are creating open, clean spaces which are calming and visually pleasing.

Only Bedroom Items in the Bedroom

This may seem like a very obvious statement but overtime everyone has objects that migrate into their bedrooms that are simply not supposed to be there. Personally, dirty dishes and glasses from a late night bedtime snack always seem to be the items that creep into my bedroom when really they should be in the dishwasher.

These items are different for everyone but we all know what should and shouldn't be there. After figuring out what item or items seem to be vacationing in your bedroom kick them out! This step is extremely easy but will be very helpful in eliminating dirt and stressors from your space.

Kick the Trash to the Curb.

Old receipts, clothes tags, magazines, newspapers, wrappers, and other pieces of paper are one of the quickest things to pile up anywhere in a home but in a bedroom they cause a lot of unnecessary piles and stress. Purchasing a trash can for your bedroom is a quick and easy fix to this problem. Just by having the trash can there you will be much more inclined to toss these items into the trash can instead of letting them pile up. Make the effort to purchase and use a trash can in your bedroom and sooner or later piles of paper will be a thing of the past for your bedroom. Empty that trash regularly and when you do, check around the room for any other items that should find their way out the door.

Avoid Tossing It

We all do it. We come into our room in a hurry and toss our jacket onto the bed and the book we were reading onto the chair but then forget to go back later and put them where they belong. Overtime these one or two tossed items add up to unmanageable proportions. Sooner or later these items will take over your room. I know it takes and extra step, but take that extra 30 seconds to hang up your jacket or put your book on the bookshelf will save yourself hours of frustration in the future. Practice this enough times and it will become a habit and won't feel like such a chore.

Minimize the Throw Pillows and Accessories

Look at any display of bedding and you will see a multitude of decorative pillows that are positioned on the bed. It may look pretty at first glance, but each and every one of those pillows has to be removed from the bed and placed somewhere before you go to bed and then they have to be re-positioned on the bed when you make the bed. Are they really worth it? Do they add enough happiness or comfort to you that they justify the expense to buy them and then to handle a really unnecessary object. Not really. Skip this accessorizing and you will be glad you did.

A jewelry box and potentially some other personal item or framed photographs are really the only things that should find a spot on top of your dressers. A good night lamp, book or a glass of water is nice for the night table. Keep furniture top items to a minimum and your bedroom will be easier to clean and much more restful.

Take a few minutes to complete these steps in your bedroom each and every day. You will immediately notice the difference. You will sleep better at night, feel happier in the morning, and be able to love relaxing in your organized bedroom. You will not be disappointed!

CHAPTER 17

CLOSETS AND WARDROBES

There is nothing like a bedroom closet that can either bring us great satisfaction or send chills through our spine. Before we can really dig in, we must admit something to ourselves. Our closets are often overfilled and messy, nothing like the picture perfect closets we see in magazines or dream about.

There never seems to be enough space to put all of our favorite blouses, jackets, jeans, and most importantly our treasured shoes. Chances are you have also stuffed other non-clothing items into your closet. So now the clothing you really need to get out of your closet are crammed in with everything else we own.

Like every other thing we have addressed in this book, you need to determine what is really necessary, makes your life less stressful and frees up time to do more important things.

With organizing closets, I have found that there really is no starting in bite-size pieces. The better option is to set aside a reasonable amount of time and tackle your whole closet. While this may seem like a daunting task, the results will be worth it. You can easily save yourself 15 minutes each morning, by decluttering and organizing your closet that only takes an hour or two on one weekend or evening.

1. Take everything out of your closet. You need to clearly be able to see what you have. The only realistic way to do this is to take all of the items in your closet out and place them somewhere big and open. I found my bed or the coffee table seems to do the trick. This may seem a lot of unnecessary work to take it all out just to put it all back in later. However, you won't know what to eliminate and then to subsequently organize if you don't know everything that is hiding in the deep dark corners of your closet.

2. Sort your clothing by category. By sort I mean putting jeans in a jean pile, sweaters in a sweater pile, workout clothes in a workout pile, etc. It becomes enormously helpful later if you take the time to make these piles neat and folded or hang the items on hangars. Do not just pile them into giant heaps of fabric. Dividing your items up into categories makes it much easier to get a big picture of all of the things you have including the things you might have forgotten about.

3. Make sure it all fits. Each item you decide to keep and return to your closet should be necessary, fit your body and your current lifestyle. Realistically, why keep pair of jeans or a cardigan that doesn't fit anymore or that doesn't fit our personal style today.

This step in relatively easy, won't take much time, and will help filter out pieces of clothing that there is no reason to put back into your closet.

To start, try on the clothes you haven't worn in a while and check to see if they are still the right size and style for your body. Overtime, all of our body sizes change and it is easy to forget that a shirt which fit 5 years ago might not fit now.

After trying everything on, if things still fit, you can honestly say you will wear them and are worth taking up space in your closet, go ahead and keep them for now. But if they don't fit, don't flatter your figure, or don't fit your lifestyle it is time to say goodbye and move them into a donation box or sell them.

4. Don't keep a bunch of repeats. Overtime some repeat pieces begin to pile up since we tend to be drawn to similar items while shopping. For me it always seems to be that I end up with 5 black t-shirts or way too many brown tank tops.

After organizing what you have in step one, it should be easy to see a pattern of what pieces you have been stock piling. Once you have identified repeat groups, identify one or two items that you want to keep from each and send the rest to the donation box. It is ok to keep some repeats of course, especially the ones you use the most often but hoarding a lifetime supply of white sweaters is not only senseless but also space filling.

Not to sound cliché, but this step really is like killing two birds with one stone. First it will help open up space in your closet and more importantly it will make choosing what to wear in the morning far simpler when you only have one option to select.

5. Think about what you wear and need. Take a second to think about your lifestyle right now and then take a look back at your clothes. Do the types of clothes you have match the needs of the activities you take part in? For example, do you still have the skin tight, low cut, way to short dress you wore in college to go out on a Friday night but really have no appropriate use for this dress anymore. Do you live in Arizona now but still have a bunch of wool sweaters from when you lived in Minnesota?

For years I kept suits, dresses and shoes that I needed for management level job I held in a Fortune 100 Company. I loved those clothes and had spent several dollars acquiring them. It took me some time and some soul-searching questions, to make me realize that I wouldn't be wearing many of those items anymore. It didn't matter what I once felt about them – that job was in the past – and I had no intentions of returning to that lifestyle. While it was ok to keep a few of these items for certain occasions, they clearly didn't warrant the space it took up in my closet. Certainly someone else could use and appreciate these items more that I could. In doing so, I was able to also help someone else – a double benefit.

If you run into situations like this, it is probably time to get rid of some of these pieces that you will most likely not wear again. Sometimes this can be hard to admit but it is amazing how much room in your closet these senseless items can take up.

6. Give priority to staples. This time repeats are good. However, by repeat I mean items in your closet that can be worn with more than one outfit. The majority of the time these items are staple items such as jeans, black flats, off-white tops, and that little black dress which can easily be mixed and matched with other clothes to create unique looking outfits. These pieces are the foundation for a great wardrobe and should make up the bulk of the things in your closet.

Take a look at the all of the clothes you have laid out. Do the majority of them match these criteria or do you have a lot of items that are a one outfit item? If you seem to have a lot of staples that is great and you probably don't need to spend too much time on this step but if not you have some work to do. The work should start with figuring out what types of outfits you wear the most and which items are used to create that look. All of the clothing pieces that fall into an outfit multiple times are good to keep but anything that doesn't should be sorted through carefully.

It is entirely fine to have a few statement or unique pieces that you want to keep like a special dress for going out or a specially patterned shirt that can only be worn once in a while. These items are necessary to not be boring but should not consume a lot of space.

After you have realistically sorted through which items are useful put anything leftover into the donation box. This step can be pretty hard but it is a vital point in making your closet organized and useable.

7. Sort by seasons. By this point you should have done a pretty good job weeding through what is going to stay and what needs to move on which means it is time to consider putting things away again. Your entire goal is to keep your closet from getting cluttered or hard to use. One of the easiest ways to do this is to sort your clothes by the season.

If you are organizing your closet during the summer put only the items you wear now into your closet not all of those bulky winter sweaters that absorb so much room. Likewise if it is winter, you probably will not need to have shorts easily accessible each morning but would much rather need some warm scarves. This idea works for all seasons: summer, fall, winter, spring, and everything that may fall in between.

The clothing that you won't be wearing in the current season should be placed into storage – not your closet – until it is time to swap out your clothes for the next season. I have found that plastic storage containers that fit under a bed or vacuum bags work great and are still easy enough to access if you decide to take a mid-winter vacation to a warm weather climate. By putting away all the clothes that you don't need right now you will save massive amounts of room in your closet.

8. Put the items you want and need back neatly. Finally after all of your hard work it is time to put everything back into your closet! After all the work you have done thus far, don't have it all go to waste by slumping everything back into your closet. Instead take time to create an organizational system or use the one you already have if it works.

9. Start It – Test It – Use It. There is no single system that will work for everybody but it is vital to find one that works for you. More importantly is to a system one that you can maintain so that you can keep the dream closet you worked so hard to obtain for a long time.

The kind of basic organization that needs to be in almost every closet is to have clothes hanging or folded neatly; categorized by purpose and type; sorted by season; off of the floor; and in baskets or shoe boxes on the shelves. Beyond this, if you find a system that works well for you by all means use it.

There are no precise rules. What is most important is that you **start it, test it, find something that works** for you, and **use it**.

This nine step plan makes it so easy and manageable for you to get your closet in order that now getting ready in the morning or for a night out will feel like a breeze. It is just great to wake up every morning to a hassle free closet.

PART FIVE

INTANGIBLES

> The biggest room in the world is the room for improvement.
> — Japanese Proverb

CHAPTER 18

TIME MANAGEMENT

Daily life consists of making choices about performing various tasks, but you may feel bogged down if you do not impose a limit. If you cultivate the viewpoint that it is impossible to do everything in one day, you may find that you have the extra time in which you can actually enjoy your life.

Understanding your priorities can make your lifestyle simpler and less cluttered. Your elimination of physical clutter is only one accomplishment. You now need to eliminate scheduled chores, meetings and activities that fit into the clutter category.

Determine Your Priorities

Determining daily priorities is easier when you understand that your life has a spiritual significance. While you do need to make sure your home is clean and organized, you also must nurture your inner being. A soul that is not nurtured gradually dies, and you are left with an empty shell consumed by cluttered tasks.

Make a list of priorities that do not focus solely on washing floors, doing your laundry and cleaning out the refrigerator. Divide your mundane chores into five scheduled days of work, leaving two days free for rest and relaxation.

Avoid Scheduling too many Household Tasks in One Day

For instance, you can decide to dust and vacuum on Monday, wash the floors on Tuesday, clean the bathroom on Wednesday and do your laundry on Thursday. Include enjoyable activities within your schedule. You can walk around the local park for one hour every Monday morning, take a yoga class every Tuesday and read a favorite book every Wednesday afternoon.

If you allow time slots for things you enjoy, your schedule will offer you a sense of freedom rather than the feeling that you are living your life within a prison consisting of mundane tasks.

Limit your Commitments

Do not make commitments that conflict with your schedule. You are not required to make unreasonable commitments that clash with your wish to live a meaningful and simple lifestyle. For instance, you do not need to feel guilty if you refuse to attend a meeting focused on a topic in which you have no real interest. If you live a lifestyle that is centered on accomplishing necessary tasks, while also allowing yourself time to participate in creative pursuits, you will have the opportunity to experience a greater degree of happiness.

Do not feel like just because you are asked to volunteer at a school, church or community function that you need to respond affirmatively. While it is fine to volunteer, don't let volunteering become a burden. You may quickly find that if you always say yes to helping out, that you are the one they will approach all of the time to volunteer. Pause a moment and think about what that commitment will cause you to give up in another area of your life.

Often in work situations, it seems like there are meetings scheduled for the sake of scheduling a meeting. It is definitely ok to pose the question whether or not you will accomplish valuable tasks or learn a lot by participating. If so, then by all means attend the meeting. But make sure when that before you are done that you have some takeaways or assigned next-steps that provide valuable output from the meeting.

Enjoy Spending Time with your Friends and Family

If you create a schedule that requires you to work around the clock, you will not have any time to spend with your friends, spouse or kids. Divide your day in a way that avoids the need to multitask. Since each day consists of 24 hours, the first thing you need to do is make sure your schedule includes at least eight hours of sleep every night. You can then divide the remaining 16 hours into accomplishing set goals and participating in fun activities. Remember that a workaholic lifestyle is not conducive to experiencing your life in a simple way that is free from unnecessary chores and obligations.

CHAPTER 19

MONEY MATTERS

When we have grown up in a world that is continually bombarding us with advertising messages, it is difficult to make ourselves immune to those the lifestyle and 'necessity' that are tempting us. How many times daily do we see or hear the message that this product will make us better looking, build our self-esteem, make us envied by our friends and of course...make us happy. But do they really?

Many times these portrayed feelings only provide us that satisfaction for a fleeting moment. In many cases, they actually decrease our satisfaction and happiness because we need to work harder to pay for them, increase our debt and also work to maintain them.

Quite often, after we have bought one item, we are tempted with even more advertising to get the latest model. Unfortunately, this is really a vicious cycle that in actuality doesn't make us any happier.

What we need to do is to **attack and ignore the consumerism and materialism mentality in favor of minimalism.**

This may not be easy to do since we have built this habit over many years. But we can start by making an initial review of the things we currently own or the things we have been thinking about buying. We can look at the big ticket items and the day-to-day or monthly expenses we incur. However you choose to begin, you will get on a dedicated path to simplifying your life and managing your money.

Groceries and Meals

By some accounts, eating at home can save at least 40% from your food bill. Cooking a good meal at home will also be much better for your health and wellbeing.

- Plan out your meals ahead of time. If you do this, the inadvertent stop for fast food or a restaurant meal will drop dramatically.

- Make a grocery list and stick to it. Don't overstock your pantry or refrigerator so items get lost or wasted. If you have planned your meals, this job should be easy.

- Use coupons and shop discounts when possible, but don't over-buy just because you it's on sale or you have a coupon.

- Avoid buying pre-packaged or prepared meals. Making an item from scratch at home is much less expensive.

- Grow your own. Even if you can grow a few items, such as tomatoes, carrots or fresh herbs in pots you can save significantly on groceries. Plus they will taste much better and be good for you.

- Take one month and write down what you spend on groceries and eating out. Make note of what percentage that is of your take home income. Norms for spending in the U.S. average between 9% and 12% of take home pay. However, like most of our overconsumption…we spend more of our income than most other countries on food.

- Review your food spending and budget. Look for areas to make changes.

- Cook in batches. Make a larger amount of some of your favorite recipes and make it ahead of time. Freeze the rest in meal size portions – make sure you write the date and what the item is on the container. Cooking in larger batches saves money in a number of ways; you buy in larger quantities so the price point is cheaper; you have your meals planned ahead of time so you don't have to stop for prepared food; you have your meals frozen in recommended serving sizes and therefore don't overeat. Great for saving on food budget, time and overeating.

- Buy in season and buy local. Foods in season are always less expensive and taste better too. Try shopping more frequently at your local farmers market and you will realize more savings. In most cases, locally grown foods are so much tastier that you will actually eat less and enjoy it more.

Cable, Internet and Television

Expenses for these types of items can add up very quickly. The place to start is to evaluate whether or not you really need what you are subscribing to.

- Eliminate a huge-multi-channel cable package. Do you really need or watch 250 + channels? Most of these channels are repeats or home shopping – neither one of which is ideal for spending less.

- If you really want cable, review the channels you actually watch and try to pare down to the least expensive option.

- Explore options such as Hulu, Netflix and Amazon Instant Video services that are significantly less money per month but will give you many of the programs and movie you want to watch. Local programming channels are free with an antenna set-up.

- Bundle packages for savings, eliminate unnecessary add-ons and avoid long term contracts if possible.

Phone services

- If you have a cell phone, eliminate land line phone service. I can't think of any reason you would need a land line or than for faxing documents. If that is the case, you will find much cheaper or free options elsewhere.

- Cell phones are something that can cost exorbitant dollars every month. The best option here is to realistically evaluate the options and services you need and get down to the bare minimum.

- Compare competing cell phone service providers for the best deals. Just be cautious of what they are selling you as the 'best'. This is a highly lucrative and competitive business for the providers, so they will aggressively market their services.

- Review your phone bills monthly. Look for any under or over usage or charges that don't belong to you. Make adjustments immediately.

- Cell phone carriers change their plans quite often. If you have a carrier that you intend to keep, call them periodically and ask if there is a better deal that they can offer you. We have saved more than 20 percent off of our monthly phone bill just by getting their 'current' plan. They will not automatically adjust your monthly fees downward for you unless you ask.

- Ask your employer or your carrier if they offer deals to employees of your company. Many cell phone providers offer deals for employees. This request saved us another 15 percent monthly. Every dollar you can save adds up...

Utilities

Electricity, gas, water and garbage removal are all ongoing monthly expenses and can be a huge part of housing expenses. While a portion of this is a fixed expense, there is also a huge variable portion that you can get control over.

- Turn off lights when you leave a room. I know this may sound obvious, but think about how many times you don't do this. Then think about how very simple it is to do.

- Turn off any electronics when not in use. Anything that is still plugged in, particularly with a charger, will still draw some amount of electricity even when shut off. You could try plugging these items in to a socket that is controlled by a switch in your room. Then shut the switch off to disconnect everything. Another option is to get a plug in that you can shut off the socket remotely.

- Turn down the settings to your hot water heater. Most likely there is a moderate setting that you can use and still have adequate hot water. Why keep heating water that you are not going to use.

- Some municipalities will give you a break on your electric bill if you agree to let them limit your service during peak times. Contact your local service provider. I have used this option for years and only once can I remember a time where power to my air conditioning was off for a short period of time during a peak utilization period. The savings over the years has more than

- compensated for this slight inconvenience.

- If you can replace some of your appliances, make sure they have a high energy efficient rating. This is by far one of the largest ongoing savings and investments you could make.

- Be careful with your dryer usage. Drying clothes can take up a large amount of energy. Often we over-dry to our clothes, when in reality we could have set the drying time to 15 minutes or so less and still had dry clothes.

- Try not to throw everything you wear into the washer if it possibly can be worn more than once. One to two items every week can not only save energy, but time and wear and tear on you clothing.

- Any time you can save on water usage, you can save money and leave less of a footprint on our environment.

Cleaning Products

Commercial cleaning products can be very costly and unnecessary. They can also be very harsh on your possessions and the environment.

One of the best products to use for just about anything is vinegar. It is a great cleaner and very inexpensive. Mix vinegar in with warm water and add a little dish soap if needed and you are all set to go with cleaning just about anything.

However, one commercial item I do like to have around – especially in the bathroom – is the multi-use cleaning sheets that come in the small packets. Pull out one of these sheets and you can quickly clean up splattered mirrors, wipe a surface clean and disinfect small area very quickly and easily.

Eliminate Storage

Expense and excess – there is really no other way to describe most long term storage areas. If there are items that you know you will really use and need in a short period of time, then by all means store them. However, we often store items that don't fit this category at all.

Every day there are thousands of abandoned long term storage units that are auctioned off to potential buyers. Why? Well either people can no longer afford them, die, or decide they really don't want or need the items in storage. If they had dealt with these items much earlier, they could have eliminated unnecessary expenses that were for items that they don't even want or remember they had.

One of the most extreme and sad cases I have seen of hoarding and storage use comes from a friend of mine. She has graciously allowed a homeless person, whom she found sleeping in his vehicle on her property, to stay on her land until he found a better living situation. As she talked to this person over time, she learned that he had multiple storage units that he kept throughout the city to store his belongings and items he had collected over the years. The gentleman was attached to these items, that he spent every dollar he had or could get from family members to pay for storage instead of having a place to live.

While many of us do not find ourselves in this situation, we need to question how dysfunctional is our actions of keeping so many of our items in storage.

Use Cash

Not much more to say here. Use cash, don't charge everything you buy. If you do charge items, make sure they only add up to the amount you can pay off every month. Then by all means, pay off your bill. Do not accumulate a credit balance. If you already have a balance built up, don't just pay off the minimum balance. You should try to pay off more of this balance every month and not purchase more until paid off.

Do It Yourself

If you haven't reviewed the services that you are paying for that you could potentially do yourself, now is the time. Do you have cleaning services and yard services? The more you simplify the less you will have to clean and maintain. You may even have more time to do some of these things yourself. If you have kids that you can engage, that is great too. It doesn't matter whether you have the money to pay for these service, simple jobs around the house build character and responsibility.

Are there other household handyman-type things that you could do also? Minor repairs, including painting, patching and simple plumbing you could learn to do. If you know how to do these things, you will save money and if you discipline yourself you can get them done immediately. Simple repairs and touchups will make you feel all the better about your surroundings.

Changing furnace filters, smoke alarm batteries and vent filters all will keep you safer and save money. We have a plan that on every Thanksgiving we change our smoke and carbon monoxide detector batteries and replace our furnace filter. It doesn't have to be that date, but pick one for you that will be an easy reminder. The advantage to this date for our family was that we often went to Grandma's house for a holiday meal. For an elderly person, it was nice to have someone else do these tasks for her. It also reminded everyone else at the gathering that it might be a good time to get this done.

Transportation

- If you can, use public transportation for routine commutes.

- Ride your bike – not only is this great for saving money but it also saves on expenses and can be a lot of fun.

- A car in many cases is a necessity, but we can make decisions about what type of vehicle is necessary and how much we spend on it.

- Look for opportunities to save on gas by eliminating unnecessary trips or consolidating your errands into one trip.

- Keeping your car well maintained will save on gas and also on costlier car repairs later.

- Do you really need a *tank* to run around in the city with? How many times do you really need an 8 passenger vehicle? All of these types of vehicles are costlier to buy and maintain.

- Review your car insurance provider and policy options. Compare your current rates with other insurance carrier rates. Periodically review your coverages to determine if you are adequately covered in a loss or are not buying excess coverage that doesn't make sense.

Bottom line is to take some time, step back and make a conscious effort to review your lifestyle and expenses. Over time you will be pleasantly surprised at your realized savings and more than surprised how much you don't miss many of these 'things'.

CHAPTER 20

LIFE IN BALANCE

Your minimalist lifestyle is not only about physical possessions. The concept of minimalism concerns intangible things as well as tangible items. Intangible necessities include living in an environment that promotes serenity, a sense of peace and good health.

Invite Serenity and Spirituality into your Life

The minimalist approach can also mean understanding the idea that your spiritual life is at stake when you do not water the seeds of your soul. Lack of spirituality in your life could either be due to focusing on physical stuff you do not really need to own or dwelling on outer activities to the extent that you lose all sense of inner peace and harmony.

It is easy to immerse yourself in tangible items that cause you to disconnect with the deepest part of yourself. You can lose a sense of balance in your life if you engage in destructive activities and habits.

Developing a Balanced Lifestyle

You may sometimes feel as though your life is completely out of balance. Perhaps you blame your disharmonious feelings on other people or planets. Maybe the planet associated with your astrological sun sign or rising sign is just not in the right place today. If you persist in this type of false thinking, you will create an unbalanced lifestyle. You cannot blame a lack of balance in your life on astrology. Instead of blaming your unbalanced lifestyle on an external force, look inside yourself for the real truth about your situation.

Find Out Why Your Life is Out of Balance

If your life is not in balance, you need to discover the reason for your unbalanced lifestyle. Perhaps you are dwelling on your duties to the extent that you feel overwhelmed with responsibilities. You need to find a way to remain a responsible person without losing focus on your inner self.

Your true self does not care about washing laundry or cleaning the floor. While you need to accomplish these tasks, you also must find a way to spend time getting to know your emotional and physical needs and aspirations. When you know yourself, the minimalist lifestyle you are meant to live will reveal itself to you.

Daily Affirmations

Daily affirmations are a wonderful way to change the way you feel and think about things in your life. Some people may think of daily affirmations as silly and that they do not really help. However, may people, including myself, can attest to their positive energy and positive results.

Daily affirmations work if they are tailored specifically to your own life circumstances. You should start by thinking about the negative thoughts and worries that typically can bring you down emotionally. Then, take that negative thought and turn it in to a positive statement. For example, if you find yourself thinking 'I am an unorganized person' your affirmation should become 'I am an organized person.'

Take as many of these negative thoughts as you can and right them down. Then turn each statement into a positive affirmation and write that down on another sheet of paper. Get rid of your negative statements. Daily, take the time to recite as many of these positive thoughts as you can. You can think about them, say them out loud, recite them during your commute, or sing them in the shower – whatever works for you. Just do this daily and you will find that these positive affirmations change the way you think and as a result what positive things begin to happen in your life.

Sounds simple right? Well it is. Sound corny? Try it for a month and experience the positive attitude and results you will achieve. The downside of doing this for a month is nothing…the upside is huge. What have you got to lose. I can assure you that you won't be disappointed.

Meditate

Mediation is a great tool for relaxation and stress reduction. Many individuals will start their day with meditation to relax, clear their mind, and focus their energy for the day ahead. Your emotional well-being can achieve a sense of peace and balance from meditation that is gain a new perspective, increase self-awareness, and reduces negative emotions. Doesn't this sound like a transforming way to begin or end your day.

You could meditate about how to live a minimalist lifestyle unencumbered by the temptations of the world. Take a few slow, deep breaths. Develop a grateful attitude. Make every day of your life a Thanksgiving holiday.

CHAPTER 21

ENJOY THE JOURNEY AND THE RESULTS

We have all started on this journey of living a minimalist lifestyle for varying reasons. You may have picked up this book because you want help getting simplifying and decluttering. You may have wanted to new skills to help you get organized and make positive changes in your life. Or perhaps, you were looking for ways to reduce the stress in your life and live more simply.

Whatever your reason for reading this book, I sincerely hope that you have picked up some new skills, gained some new ideas and have realized that minimalism isn't an impossible or unachievable lifestyle. I hope you have also realized that there are many spectrums of minimalism and you can work to achieve a balance that works for you.

With all the complexities we face in today's world, isn't it refreshing to know that we can actually do something to reduce our stress and simplify our life. Just imagine how you will feel with more joy, balance and meaning in your life.

Don't get paralyzed – just get started with simplifying, decluttering and getting organized – your sense of well-being will be the first to tell you that this is working for you... So here's to you...

Define Your Needs

Get Motivated

Develop New Habits

Declutter and Simplify

Enjoy the Journey

Embrace Life

You are well on your way to less stress, more fulfillment from life and the personal satisfaction that comes from achieving your goals.

ABOUT THE AUTHOR

Karen Alexander is an author, a mother, a passionate chef, and a serial entrepreneur. She left the corporate world, after many years, to spend time with family and pursue her many interests. She has spent the last decade cultivating these passions, many relating to home, food and health. She writes about many of these topics.

Her books are designed to help people find inspiration and answers to questions they have in everyday life. She is an exhaustive researcher and has hands-on experience with the topics she covers.

She currently lives in Madison, WI

From the Author:

Thank you very much for reading this book about Minimalism. I know your time is valuable. I hope you gained something from reading this book, particularly how living simple can change your life. My hope is that you will give the steps here an honest attempt. My hunch is that you will pleasantly amazed with the positive changes.

Would You Do Me A Quick Favor?

If you liked this book and found it particularly helpful, I would really appreciate it if you left a review on Amazon. Your support on Amazon means a lot to me! It really helps me out, and I read every single review.

Made in the USA
Lexington, KY
19 January 2014